THE AVIATOR'S TOILET COMPANION

ALMOST TWENTY PRECISELY TRUE STORIES, SENSITIVELY SELECTED
SOME FOR SHORT SITS, AND SOME FOR LONG SITS

WRITTEN AND ILLUSTRATED BY

ROB OWEN

Publisher: Rob Owen. P O Box 4232, Durbanville. 7551. Western Cape. RSA. Email: robowenart@gmail.com
dungpublishing@gmail.com

ISBN Print: 978-0-620-78790-1
ISBN e-Book: 978-0-620-78791-8

DUNG PUBLISHING
WE ROLL IT AROUND
©

AVIATOR'S TOILET COMPANION CONTENTS

INTRODUCTION

I started learning to fly in June 1971, and qualified as a private pilot in February 1972. At the time the best means of radio communication in the flight information region was by HF radio, and necessitated cranking out a trailing wire aerial attached to a drogue in the form of a plastic funnel. Cranking it in again was part of the vital action sequence before joining an air-field circuit. The primary means for navigation was by computing the triangle of velocities and arriving at a dead reckoning. It will be hard for the millennial pilot to reconcile this with the modern glass cockpit and GPS technology.

It will probably be equally hard to assimilate the ethos of a country in rebellion against its former colonial motherland for whom, during the Second World War, it supplied more soldiers per capita population than the motherland itself, and whose pilots earned more ace appellations than any other country in the British Empire. The Rhodesian rebel war served to bond the country's inhabitants into a unified family with a shared understanding for the necessity of risk and innovative enterprise for survival. This is by meager way of trying to explain extraordinary occurrences in extraordinary circumstances.

My wish is that this book will otherwise provide some distraction for the occasions you will be required to spend time in 'the little room'.

Rob Owen

PREFACE

There were three episodes in my flying experience which I feel impacted on it significantly.

The first was an intense three day and night, 'Advanced PPL (Private Pilot's Licence) course' with Techair Training College, two years after I had earned my PPL. The objective was to expose the participant to extreme circumstances which were not part of the required normal curriculum, but which he (or she) might encounter as a matter of necessity rather than choice. It included exercises such as maintaining a precise figure of eight pattern at low level over two landmarks not more than 200 meters apart in windy and gusty conditions, finding five objects within one hour by dead reckoning (there was no other method) after being given the coordinates, which then had to be identified after returning, and precisely following a sharply serpentine river gully at high speed.

In addition to night navigation exercises, including a VASI (Visual Approach Slope Indicator) approach to Salisbury International airport, there was a daytime exercise which involved launching 12 disparate aircraft from Piper Cubs to Beach Barons, simultaneously into the circuit, each required to maintain strict circuit protocol. This was under the precise control, and acerbic direction of Charles Prince, who became so renowned for his paternal attitude to the airport he managed, and the pilots that frequented it, that the airport was named after him. The whole course was an intense series of classroom lectures followed by one or two hour aerial exercises, from early morning into the night, and at the end of which I came away on an adrenalin high, a new attitude, and a certificate in my hand. I still recall some of these experiences with nostalgic excitement. The intention at the time was to establish this course as an annual event, but sadly it was never repeated.

The second episode was my two year stint as an 'observer' (reserve pilot) in the Police Reserve Air Wing. This was during a time when the country was supposedly at war, and when laws and rules were interpreted in terms of necessity and expedience. International sanctions imposed after a unilateral declaration of independence in 1965 had influenced the air force to set up workshops to manufacture the spares they needed for the aircraft they operated, and armaments were mounted on private aircraft by the owners, so they could perform a usefully aggressive role in the country's defense. It was a time when need dictated the means, useful innovation was given precedence over regulation, and anything was possible.

The third episode was after I conceived the notion that if you threw the pilot out of his microlight, and replaced his weight with pesticide, it would be possible to build a remotely controlled crop sprayer. After meeting Nick Hurley, Professor of electronics, the concept became a tangible ambition, and it wasn't long before we had the working model profile of a machine that would avoid obstacles, maintain a precise height above ground, measure the crosswind component related to two randomly placed beacons, and then compute its best results pattern after the field that was to be sprayed had been drawn into its interface.

It would otherwise be initially controlled by a pilot sitting on the ground behind a cathode ray (TV) screen depicting the pilot's view being transmitted from a remote front mounted camera, but also contain on board overrides for obstacle avoidance .

Nick developed the electronics; it was my job to design and build the aircraft.

In order for me to achieve this, I had to become a self taught aeronautical engineer and decide on the aerofoil that would fulfill our required performance parameters, the best means for achieving stability in all axis, learn how to manufacture propellers that would match the optimum power profile of the motor, and then to maximize the peak achievable power for the motor being tested. I must have built 30 propellers out of 6mm laminations of Yugoslavian beech, first cut from planks and then thicknessed by me.

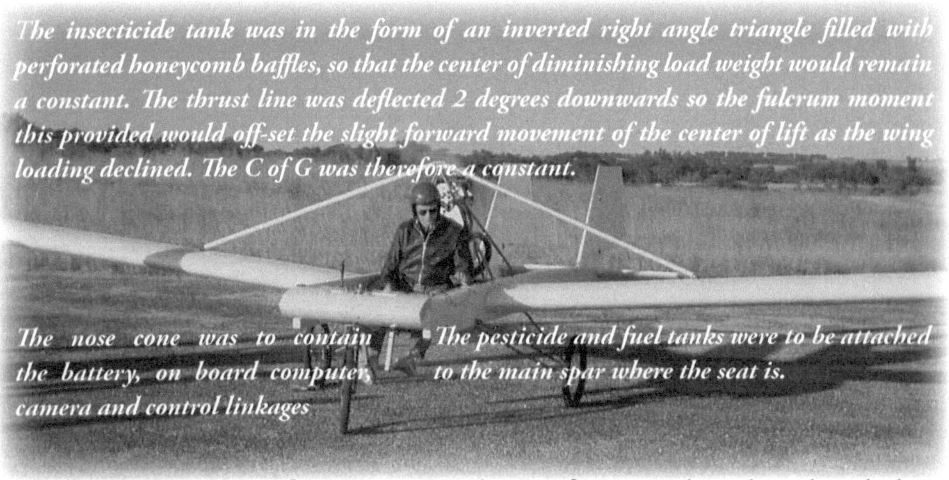
The insecticide tank was in the form of an inverted right angle triangle filled with perforated honeycomb baffles, so that the center of diminishing load weight would remain a constant. The thrust line was deflected 2 degrees downwards so the fulcrum moment this provided would off-set the slight forward movement of the center of lift as the wing loading declined. The C of G was therefore a constant.
The nose cone was to contain the battery, on board computer, camera and control linkages
The pesticide and fuel tanks were to be attached to the main spar where the seat is.

There was no source for conventional aircraft materials, other than bolts, nuts, pulleys and cable obtained from aircraft maintenance organizations, and everything else had to be substituted with what was appropriately available. This was in a country in the grip of International sanctions. The best available motor was a two stroke twin cylinder Yamaha motorcycle engine.

My tutorship for all of this was the detailed tome of A C Kermode's 'Mechanics of Flight', his 'Flight without Formula', and a Photostat copy of CAM (Civil Aeronautics Manual)18.

My motivation and enthusiasm was such that it is the only time in my life that I have stayed awake for a 72 hour stretch, spurning sleep in pursuit of my ardour. I was, after all, going to be a millionaire!

All now made laughable by drones, and GoPros.

The enterprise collapsed after Nick had to hurriedly emigrate after the new Mugabe led government was installed in 1980.

I sadly allowed my licence to lapse in August 2009, thirty eight years one month and 21 days after my very first training flight. However I hope the above particularly validates my credentials for the writing of this book.

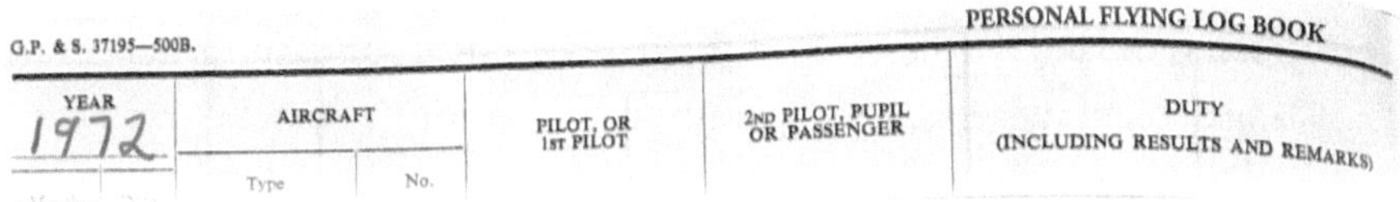

G.P. & S. 37195—500B.

PERSONAL FLYING LOG BOOK

YEAR	AIRCRAFT		PILOT, OR 1ST PILOT	2ND PILOT, PUPIL OR PASSENGER	DUTY (INCLUDING RESULTS AND REMARKS)
1972	Type	No.			

TOP HEN

In those days Umtali was a picturesque and peaceful little town, nestling between the mountains that formed the boundary between Rhodesia and Mozambique, where nothing much ever happened.

I'm not sure what the population might have been, but can say that even in its glory days, our little flying club peaked at only 27 active members.

I am certain that in line with all similar institutions, there was a hard core of these who were consistently more active than the rest, and almost without fail could be found every Saturday and Sunday, sitting around on their fold-up camping chairs, swapping lies and waiting for something to happen.

This was always under the shade of the vast Mahobohobo tree adjacent to our only hangar, where we would set up a bed of hot coals in an old horizontally cut 44 gallon drum so that all could chuck on the meat of their choice, to accompany whatever else they might have brought to constitute lunch.

Occasionally Craig would arrive with his boisterous boxer Biff, oblivious to our annoyance (since everyone was too polite to tell him).

Biff would immediately bound out of the back of Craig's pick-up and head for a flock of chickens from a nearby village that were in the habit of scratching around the cleared area which we liked to think of as our airfield apron.

A chaotic and offensive cacophony of squawking and flapping would follow, resulting in the whole flock being huffily lined up along the support rail above the open hangar door, all puffed up and clucking their annoyance whilst they recovered their dignity.

It was as a result of this established convention that on a particularly hot and sonorous Saturday following Biff's arrival, a profound and intellectual debate was provoked regarding the evolution of the domestic hen, and a comparison of its flying capability to that of other examples of the fowl genus. Naturally there was technical comparison between the domestic hen and ubiquitous wild Guinea fowl (colloquially referred to as spotted chickens).

Ray pointed out that the chicken's more vertical tail feathers, whilst perhaps assisting with lateral axis and directional control, could not be utilised as advantageously as the Guinea Fowl's more elevator like arrangement for longitudinal pitch control, critically important for such low aspect ratio stubby wings. This was particularly since the wings also provided the thrust. Billy postulated that this argument was precisely why the opposite was more relevant.

The dispute became sufficiently heated for a number of us to be goaded into catching a member of the local flock, so that Ross could fling it up as high as possible from the apex of the hangar roof.

He was determined to prove that, according to his sworn claim of having previously witnessed this behaviour, the chicken would fix its wings in glide mode and be capable of establishing an acceptable ratio when faced with the prospect of an extended flight.

Momentarily, between an hysterically flapping start and similarly flapping finish, there was only a fleeting interlude when it did appear to be gliding, but too briefly to quell the jeering doubters, and this only served to cause even more intense argument.

Consequently, a short while later found three of us labouring up to ten thousand feet in the Cessna 172 with one of the doors off, and Ross on the back seat clutching a chicken, with what seemed to be an anticipatory gleam in its eye.

Sadly, despite Billy's exemplary execution of a maximum-rate 180° turn immediately following the moment of release, there was no sight of anything but a few drifting feathers, and our attempt at scientific closure was wasted. (Take into account that before entry into the turn he had reduced the speed to a state where the stall warning was a constant wail with 40 degrees of flap selected, so that the chicken would not be too severely buffeted on departure.)

Before, good reader, you might be inclined to accuse us of too callous and cruel behaviour, let me relate that on the following Sunday morning, unmistakably the same chicken was strutting up and down the top centre section of the Cessna wing, seemingly waiting to go again, and judging from the respectful gaze of the rest of the flock, had been significantly elevated in the pecking order.

In fact, for some considerable time, there was the nuisance of having to wash chicken shit from the top of the wing, until apparently the day arrived for Top Hen's turn in her owner's pot.

Learning the secret of flight from a bird was a good deal like learning magic from a magician. After you know what to look for, you see things that you did not notice when you did not know exactly what to look for.

Orville Wright

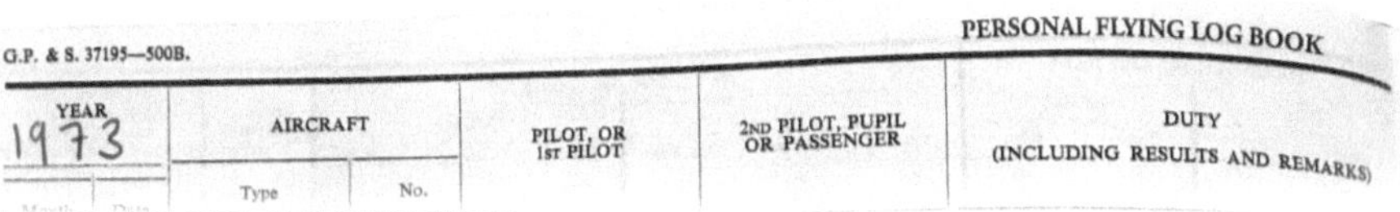
G.P. & S. 37195—500B.
PERSONAL FLYING LOG BOOK

YEAR 1973	AIRCRAFT Type / No.	PILOT, OR 1st PILOT	2nd PILOT, PUPIL OR PASSENGER	DUTY (INCLUDING RESULTS AND REMARKS)

SOLO CROSS COUNTRY

I don't remember his name; - it was a long time ago.

I do remember that he was a diligent student, who applied himself seriously in the pursuit of his PPL, and went solo with what appeared to be assured competence after the usual 12 hours or so.

This was probably after training for five or six months, because like all of us, he only flew as much as the residual of his monthly pay packet allowed.

Between flights, he was always there around the barbecue on a Saturday or Sunday afternoon. He kept pretty much to himself. I don't remember him asking for help or ever asking questions, but have no doubt that he greatly benefited from what he would learn by listening to the exploits of us veterans of as much as even a hundred hours, gathered around the cooler box.

We all took an interest in his progress because the club was so small that every member other than he, being the newest recruit, was obliged to be on the committee to comply with the legal definition. Otherwise we would only have qualified as a syndicate and not been allowed some of the necessary privileges assumed by us as a club. Like accepting 'day members' who would be flown at an hourly rate to wherever and back by a 'friend' who happened to be a legitimate member, after signing the appropriate indemnity. It is not possible to have a variance of members on a daily basis in a syndicate, and accepting payment for flying anyone anywhere as a private pilot would be illegal!

The new recruit passed his radio telephony (restricted) in due time, and we all had a hand in planning his dual cross country, as well as inviting him along when we were flying anywhere; to put in a few pointers.

Inevitably, about 18 months after he had first started flying, the day dawned for his first solo cross-country. We were all there to see him off before hauling out the skottel. We would await his return whilst breakfasting on bacon, sausage, tomatoes, mushrooms and egg, fried in the traditional style.

He never did come back.

Long after we knew that he must have run out of fuel, and had 'phoned around the places he might have been, Billy went off to the police to report the aircraft and pilot as "missing".

On Monday morning Ross 'phoned us all, to tell us that he hadn't pitched for work. They both worked in different departments of the local motor assembly plant.

On Monday evening Billy and Ross went to his flat, and were told by his landlady that she had met him coming down the stairs at around ten that morning with his suitcase in his hand. He had told her he was leaving, and that she should find another tenant. His rent was paid up.

On Tuesday morning the police 'phoned to tell us that the aircraft had been located at an airstrip about 40 nautical miles from our standard "triangle", in the eastern highlands (elevation 6,500 feet).

I drove Billy up on Wednesday afternoon to collect the aircraft, but we had to do the trip twice, because there wasn't enough fuel in the tanks to fire up the motor, a possibility we hadn't considered.

He had left on the day of his test with nearly four hours endurance and the three legs shouldn't have taken him more than an hour and a half total time. The 'plane was only 30 minutes flying time away from home.

I wonder where he went that day, and then what made him just leave like that? How did he get home? Why didn't he call one of us?

Pride I guess, - hell of a thing. It can make a man, break a man, and even kill a man!

We conjectured a lot, but never found out for sure where he went afterwards.

I wonder where he is now?

I doubt somehow, that he will get to read this.

A pilot is never lost. He might only be temporarily unsure of his precise current location.

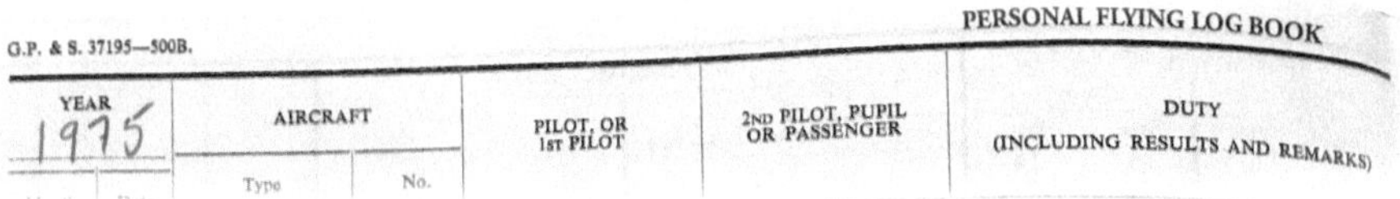
G.P. & S. 37195—500B.

PERSONAL FLYING LOG BOOK

YEAR 1975	AIRCRAFT (Type, No.)	PILOT, OR 1ST PILOT	2ND PILOT, PUPIL OR PASSENGER	DUTY (INCLUDING RESULTS AND REMARKS)

THE FICKLE FINGER OF FATE

The crop spraying organization that Ian worked for had stationed him with his crop sprayer at the then recently established Middle-Sabi intensive irrigation scheme which was expanding at a phenomenal rate.

As soon as the summer crop was harvested, the ground was prepared for winter wheat, and again, the contract ploughing teams went in right behind the Combine Harvesters to get the land prepared for summer cotton.

Ian's Ag-Cat was used for seeding, fertilizing, herbiciding, top dressing as well as applying a vast range of pesticides. All those so called farmers ever really had to do was drink beer while they waited for the money to roll in.

When it was necessary to submit the big Grumman for its MPI (mandatory periodic inspection), Ian was instructed to take it through to Buffalo Range, which had been extensively upgraded because of its strategic military position. He was flying back over the vast Lowveld, consisting of endless Mopani forest interspersed with numerous Baobabs sticking up out of the bush canopy like water towers, when an oil pipe feeding one of the radial cylinder heads disconnected, pumping hot oil all over his Perspex cockpit.

An unexpected bit of bad luck!

In a flash Ian released the side panel of his cockpit so he could see where he was going. Sadly, he had overlooked the possibility of a deluge of hot oil spraying straight into his eyes. Blinded, his only option was to kill the motor, before it did this all by itself, crank the trim full aft, and then slightly forward

again until the gentle buffeting induced by an impending stall disappeared, in the hope of achieving the slowest rate of descent; and try to keep the wings level.

Eyes burning, and with only a vague blur when he forced one open to a slit, he did his best to keep the ball in the middle with rudder, tightened his harness as much as he could, and anxiously waited for impact.

The next thing he was aware of was the bumping of his wheels as they trundled across the surface of the only salt pan in 100 square miles. The aircraft had floated down and flared in its own ground effect.

Incredible good fortune!

Mindful of the fact that he was drenched with oil and there was a potential fire hazard, he blindly scrambled out of the cockpit on to the wing.

Being a tail dragger (so the wings were presented at a high angle of attack), and the wing made slippery with oil, his feet shot out from under him, and he fell head first over the leading edge. His head hit a protruding rock, and he was badly concussed.

An unfortunate accident!

Incredibly, in that remote and inhospitable place, and at the height of the bush war, his descent had been observed by a patrolling military unit some miles away, who then found and rescued him, and he soon recovered.

An extraordinary chance of providence!

Sadly, some weeks later he suffered a mild 'blackout' for a few moments. This happened a number of times over the next few months, and finally his licence was rescinded on medical grounds.

A tragic consequence!

When fate whimsically waggles her fickle finger, there is just no foretelling what the final outcome might be.

Like the winds of the sea are the ways of fate. As we voyage along through life. 'Tis the set of the soul that decides the goal, and not the calm of the strife.

Ella Wheeler Wilcox - Winds of Fate.

G.P. & S. 37195—500B. PERSONAL FLYING LOG BOOK

YEAR 1973	AIRCRAFT		PILOT, OR 1ST PILOT	2ND PILOT, PUPIL OR PASSENGER	DUTY (INCLUDING RESULTS AND REMARKS)
	Type	No.			

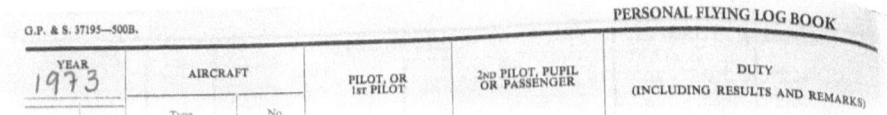

INSTRUCTOR FROM HELL

Those beer-swilling settlers down in the remote Middle-Sabi lowveld had been making so much money that buying private aircraft, and getting their PPLs had become the new cult.

As a consequence, our little flying club, the only one within a two hundred and fifty kilometers radius, had grown from depending solely on the old Piper Colt for the past seven years, to a Cessna 172 and then a Cherokee 180. All achieved in the previous twelve months.

It was obvious we were now going to need a full time instructor. We could then leave him with one of the aircraft down at Middle-Sabi to generate even more income during the week.

Billy, our chief instructor and chairman, conducted the interviews, and despite his carefully cultivated posture of Fonze nonchalance, seemed a little awed by his new recruit.

Frank was a wonder boy. He had joined the air force aged 17, and had done time on Hunters as well as Allouetes amongst a number of other accomplishments. He had been the youngest ever to achieve something, but I can't remember what it was, and then left after his five year contract expired because he felt there was more potential in the commercial arena. Suffice it to say that by the time we employed him aged only 23, he already had his commercial licence, and full instructor's rating.

So on the very first Friday afternoon after he had joined us, we were off down to Middle Sabi for a full weekend of instruction. Billy in the 172, and Ross and I with Frank, in the Cherokee.

When we reached the lowveld proper, there were a number of isolated active cumuli-nimbus clouds, but interspersed with blue sky, and nothing to be too concerned about.

That is until Frank asked, "Hey, have you guys ever been in a thunderstorm?" immediately following which the nose was pointed towards the nearest cloud.

There was just enough time whilst we were being sucked towards this roiling dark mass at an unbelievable ground speed, for me to sit on my hands to prevent them from involuntarily being whacked against the roof and elsewhere in the initial turbulence. There certainly wasn't opportunity to

ask Frank whether he understood the structural variance between a military fighter jet and a Piper Cherokee!

To describe what followed is beyond my limited literary ability. We were suddenly in a roaring world of blackness, blue, blinding white and glowing orange, pervaded with the smell of fear and sulphur.

One moment my head was extended on a bungee, the next being crushed into my shoulders with a grunt, or perhaps it was a scream, I didn't care. There was no time for introspective reflection, but only for intense praying, before we were suddenly spewed out, wet and shiny into brilliant sunshine. The new opportunity for visual reference was still limited by there being three of everything, due to the turbulence.

When it was sufficiently calm for me to be aware that Ross was looking at me, I saw raw terror, which I knew I was reflecting, and in that instant I think we tacitly conspired never to tell anyone. Frank wore a maniacal grin.

It was a relief to be flying back on Sunday afternoon, having left Frank behind with the 172 to instruct farmers for a two-week stint.

About three weeks after his return, Frank landed with some telephone lines trailing from the Cherokee fin, where the rotating beacon had recently been, and even before the Postmaster General had advised he intended suing for damages, we knew we had no alternative but to summarily fire him.

Frank shrugged it off, admitting to having already responded to a recruitment brochure for the British Royal Air Force. His application was successful, and someone told me just a few years later that he had been selected to join the Red Arrows aerobatic team.

After his departure, his pupil confessed that on the day of the telephone wire incident, they had impacted the wires that crossed the railway track while playing chicken with an oncoming train.

I knew Frank had left a legacy when I saw Rupert, a Middle Sabi settler, doing barrel rolls on long final in his newly acquired Tripacer, shortly after Billy sent him on his first solo.

I haven't heard of Frank since; whether he is dead yet, but I would think he must be by now.

There are Old pilots, and there are Bold pilots, but there are no Old Bold pilots.

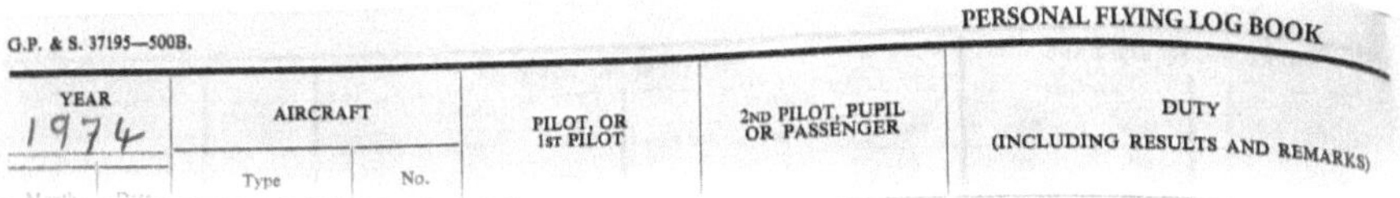
G.P. & S. 37195—500B.

PERSONAL FLYING LOG BOOK

YEAR	AIRCRAFT		PILOT, OR 1ST PILOT	2ND PILOT, PUPIL OR PASSENGER	DUTY (INCLUDING RESULTS AND REMARKS)
1974	Type	No.			

LIKE FATHER LIKE SON

"Another beer?" asked Andre.

"That would be great," I responded.

Andre got up to execute this errand, and I heard his muffled conversation from the kitchen where our two wives were now knocking together a potluck supper. We had dropped in earlier for a supposedly quick late Sunday afternoon visit. Naturally the conversational hangar doors had opened, and we had become involved in matters aviation which had stretched the afternoon past sundowners.

With Andre's temporary absence, my attention became focused on the antics of little Frankie, who was swooping and buzzing noisily around the open-plan dining room next door, clasping a beautifully detailed scale model of a Cessna 172, the type in which Andre was doing his ab-initio training. This one was even painted in the same livery.

"Just like Andre," I thought. He always embraced whatever he was doing with unbounded enthusiasm, and after taking up his long-time dream of learning to fly, he had wanted to solicit his family's complicity so that they could share his experience.

His wife, Lorraine was already very actively involved with the catering and social arrangements at the flying club, while Frankie often rode shotgun during his Dad's training sessions.

Andre had been complaining however, that he was becoming a little frustrated that his instructor had not considered him competent to go solo after nearly 18

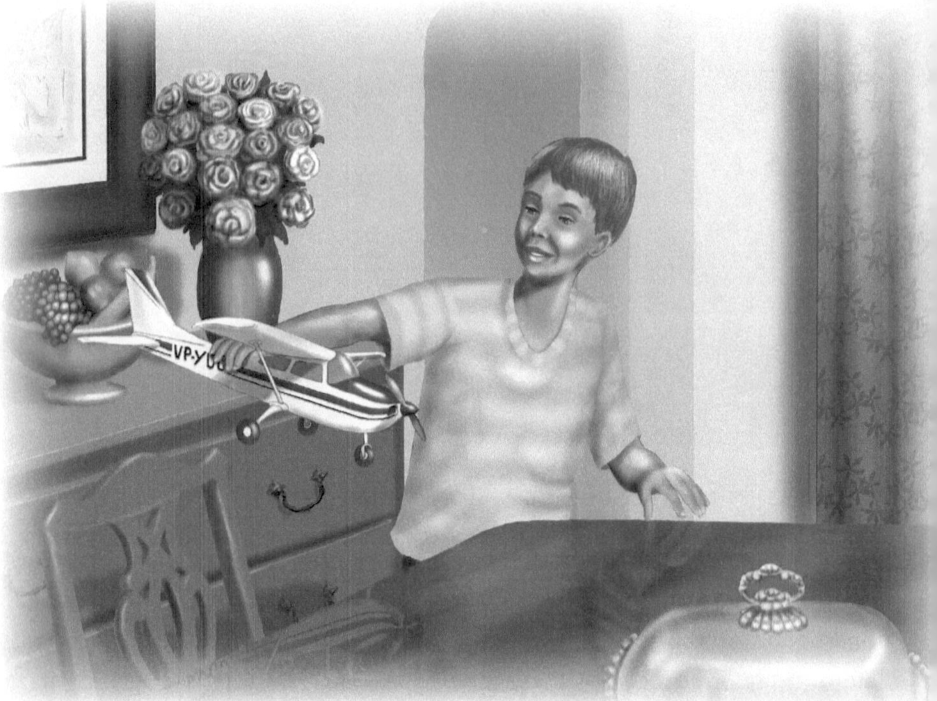

hours of dual, and was beginning to suspect that this might be influenced by some money making agenda, aimed at extracting the maximum revenue. The hourly rate for dual was much higher than that for solo, and was structured to cover the contracted commercial instructor's fee. Andre probably had a point. We were a very small club, badly in need of new members, and he was probably the only one under instruction at the time.

"Vrrrrrrrrrrr, Control, Control" demanded little Frankie. " Vrrrrrrrrrrrr, Yes Cessna, Cessna, this is control, what do you want? Vrrrrrrrr." "Vrrrrrrrr, Cessna, Cessna permission to land over, vrrrrrrr. You are cleared left turn for straight in approach, vrrrrrr."

At this point little Frankie lined up for the dining room table, descending on a perfect glide slope for the nearest longitudinal edge.

I had to see the outcome of this approach and I was riveted. Just above the surface, the nose of the scale model suddenly tilted up, and the monotone vrrrrrrrrrr was interrupted with a 'kapow' simultaneously accompanied by slamming the scale model down on the table top, followed by a bounce and another ‘kapow’, after several of which there was a ‘screeeee’ to denote the screeching of tyres, followed by the model slewing to a halt.

Andre plonked my fresh beer beside me, and collapsed into his chair with his.

“Any trouble with your landings, Andre?” I enquired.

His head jerked up guiltily. “They are not always perfect, but who has perfect landings every time?” was all he replied. A tad defensively, I thought.

There are two types of aeroplanes; those that you fly, and those that fly you. You must have a distinct understanding from the very first as to who is the boss.

Ernest K Gann

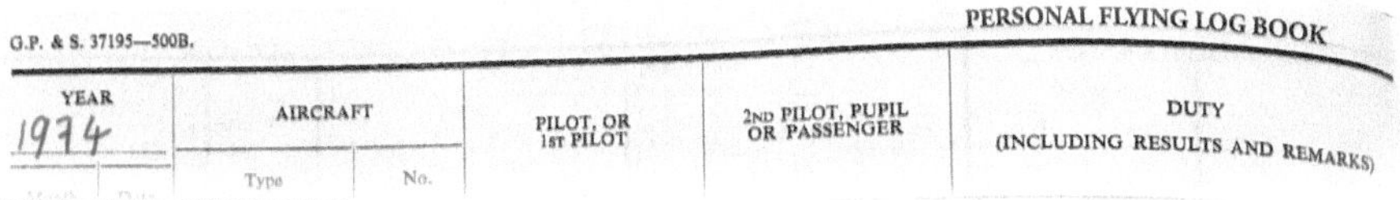
G.P. & S. 37195—500B.

PERSONAL FLYING LOG BOOK

YEAR	AIRCRAFT		PILOT, OR 1ST PILOT	2ND PILOT, PUPIL OR PASSENGER	DUTY (INCLUDING RESULTS AND REMARKS)
1974	Type	No.			

A SINFUL THING

Whoomph!

I felt my breath go out, and was aware of Ross sucking in air with a whistle after he had elbowed me in the ribs with unnecessary force. It had the desired heads-up effect though, to be met with the vision of

Mrs Gregory Murray.

It really isn't fair to be making commandments about not coveting your neighbour's wife, and then allowing DNA to metamorphose into this result.

Greg was walking towards Billy, our club Chairman and instructor, with the obvious intention of introducing her, whilst her green eyes flashed her appraisal of each us motley lot in turn, oblivious of our gaping mouths. We, on the other hand, were nervously apprehensive that raw lust might become a visible phenomenon.

Greg had joined the Club and been learning to fly for perhaps the last six months, during which time the AGM had taken place, and he had been elected to the club committee as treasurer.

This was an obvious consequence of the fact that he was a Chartered Accountant, and financial officer for the biggest corporation of which our little town could boast.

We had wondered why Greg had never previously brought his wife up to the flying club, and I suppose had assumed that she probably was just not the flying club type. In retrospect now though, it must have been that he felt insecure, and did not wish to invite any potential competition for her attention. He was a big clumsy guy with a cherubic face behind horn rimmed spectacles, and it would have been less than honest to describe him as good looking.

Today was different though. They had arrived in a brand new Jaguar XJ6, and there was a bundle of expensive looking camera cases hanging round Greg's portly neck, which he managed to wear with a kind of swagger. His wife seemed to flout the impression that she was newly glinting.

Recognizing the obvious need to explain this new ostentation, Greg revealed that he had been left a substantial legacy by an old forgotten Aunt in England, and then proudly announced that he had ordered a brand new Cherokee Six 300.

Now that he was the center of attention, we suddenly noticed what a fine fellow he was, and warmed to him considerably.

This warmth increased particularly after his Cherokee Six arrived, and he allowed those of us that he considered to be true friends, to convert to it.

With Greg's newfound self-esteem, his wife was now a frequent participant in club activities, but ogling of her magnificent charms was only conducted with utmost discretion, for fear of displeasing the sharer of all this good fortune.

There was seemingly no end to his munificence, and just a few weeks after the arrival of his Cherokee 6, he donated a second-hand Cherokee 180 to the club.

Those were happy days.

Until one Saturday morning, after we had habitually arrived at the airfield to discover that the sheriff had strung securely padlocked lengths of chain around the undercarriage of all the aircraft, and pasted prohibition notices on the side windows.

After his arrest, it took seven months for the police to complete their forensic accounting in order to establish the extent to which Greg had been laundering

his conversion of corporate funds through the club books; during which there was of course no activity, and no revenue being earned to pay the installments on the 172.

After Greg was convicted, the sheriff took the two Cherokees, the bank took the 172, and we were left with just the original little Colt, and a bunch of unpaid bills.

We must learn from this; that a beautiful woman can bring a flying club to ruination, and that coveting a fellow club member's wife is a definite no-no. It can certainly evoke the wrath of the sheriff.

Oh yes: and that an accountant can be a crook.

You have got to expect that things are going to go wrong, and we always need to prepare ourselves for the unexpected.

Neil Armstrong

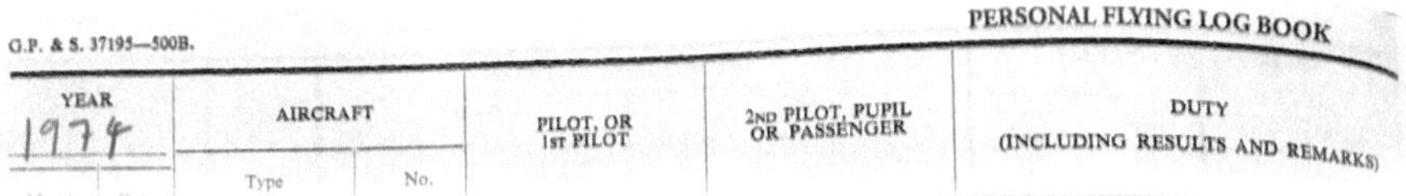

EMERGENCY RE-FUELLING FACILITIES

Auntie Joan was always very fond of telling us that "nothing in God's kingdom is ever lost". If she were still around, I would challenge her to find the anti-rattle spring that zinged off the calipers while I was changing the brake pads on my pick-up. This was on an open area of concrete outside the workshop door, and every morning for the next three years when I arrived to unlock, I could not overcome the obsessive compulsion to look around for that damned spring. It had to be there!

Thank goodness I subsequently moved on to new premises.

This is by way of explaining why I still keep my old Rhodesian Aeronautical Information Publication (AIP).

It was almost certainly my first serious post PPL cross-country and I am sure I must have planned it in great detail. One hour fifty minutes each way with no wind, and four and a half hours endurance, leaving forty-five minutes reserve.

The visit to my parents with my girlfriend was primarily to demonstrate how rewarding their procreative efforts had turned out, now that there was a PILOT in the family, and I am certain the weekend was spent with me insufferably pronouncing on all things aeronautical whilst my father smoked his pipe and my mother responded with "yes dear".

Submission of flight plans before departure was strictly compulsory for all flights in Rhodesia, even from one farm strip to another, and the return trip was planned with much flourishing of maps, my Airtour CRP 1 computer, and products of Jeppesen Sanderson Inc. all over the dining room table. (My father was probably a bit piqued by the fact that the eminence of his Masonic rituals was being so challenged, but then he had enjoyed all the glory for too long.)

After phoning Met, my parents took us up to the local Municipal airstrip to see us off after lunch on Sunday.

The regional air traffic was controlled by Thornhill Military, and soon after establishing climb-out, I announced my estimate for the TMA boundary on the Thornhill approach control frequency, being somewhat surprised when they responded, because the Military usually closed down after 13:00hrs on weekends. It was now after 14:00, but there had probably been a few Air Force students still bumbling around in the Provosts they used for their ab-initio training.

My estimate for the boundary for the little Piper Colt would have been around 25 minutes, and after 30 the air traffic controller, sounding a little peeved, came on air to ask whether I was there yet! The last of his students had probably long gone home to roost by then, and he was now becoming anxious to get home for his Sunday lunch and a cold beer, but felt he needed to make sure I was out of his control space first, so that he could then hand me over to Salisbury Information and absolve himself of any further responsibility for me.

When he called, my anxiety had become at least equal to his. For some time I had begun to suspect that things weren't altogether going to plan after running neck and neck with a blue station wagon with two bicycles and a TV on the roof carrier, traveling on the main tar road to Umvuma, which ran parallel to my track. The station wagon had been edging ahead. I had been mentally wrestling with the burden of trying to compute a revised estimate, but the fact that we had only just flown over the airfield at Lalapanzi, which was only two thirds the distance to the terminal boundary, was more than I could immediately come to terms with, and my brain had become somewhat addled. I was beginning to doubt all my efforts at the dining room table, even wondering whether perhaps I had been using the wrong scale.

"Reporting your boundary out at this time," I spontaneously lied, knowing that he would almost certainly close shop and I might then avoid the certainty that he would end up considering me an idiot, and I would be left alone to

sort out my predicament without further loss of dignity.

It was another ten minutes before we were overhead the river that identified the terminal boundary, by which time I had come to the realization that I must be flying into a considerable head wind, and that at this rate, there was no way I would reach my destination with the available fuel.

I remember my indignation and anger directed at MET (meteorological forecast for Aviation), but you will understand that I was very inexperienced at the time, and had yet to learn that this service was only established with the hope that at some future time they might get it right.

A despairing search of the map confirmed that there was no re-fuelling alternative closer than my destination, and I wondered if it was possible to arrange for fuel if I returned to my departure aerodrome, certain however that this would be a lost cause.

I was getting into a sweat, and decided I just needed time to think this thing out, so turned around to land back at Lalapanzi. I was there in seven minutes, which clearly demonstrated that I had been flying into a head wind of over 30 knots!

Once back on the ground, I hauled out my AIP, and was leafing through the pages desperate for inspiration.

This is when I suddenly saw an entry that read; 'Thornhill Restricted Military Airport – emergency re-fuelling only.'

Well I didn't need any further prompting, and with lightened heart was hustling my girlfriend back into the Colt, so that within a minute or two we were once again in the air, and with a 35 knot tail wind it was only a short while later I was making advisory calls to an unresponsive Thornhill Tower, before landing.

After turning off at the first taxi opportunity, we came across a closed multi section sliding security gate, manned by a guard and his dog. The guard was somewhat incredulous, and had obviously been warned against all manner of attempts at intrusion, except perhaps, a little aircraft with a pilot pointing at a thick green manual demanding petrol, and was persuaded to let us in.

Logically, an aerodrome is, after all, a place for aeroplanes.

As it turned out, the dog, which was in a frenzy of barking and bearing its teeth, seemed to have a better grip on the situation, because an hour later, we were under arrest for contravention of the 'Official Secrets Act', under the 'Emergency Power Regulations'.

I had been trying desperately during that time to explain my arrival in terms of the concession regarding emergency re-fuelling, but had not been able to find this anywhere.

This was after all, a country supposedly at war, and whilst I had been feverishly flashing through the pages of the AIP, it had begun to dawn just how deep in the dwang we now were. It had to be there, I saw it with my own eyes.

But it wasn't.

I still look for it. Still can't find it.

So if there is a pilot 'up there' as a result of being the victim of perhaps misreading an approach plate because he was so anxious to see what he wanted to, please find Auntie Joan (She will be in the intake registry for June, 1993), and ask her why if "nothing in God's Kingdom is ever lost", then how is it possible to find things that were never there!

The only time an aeroplane has too much fuel on board is when it is on fire.

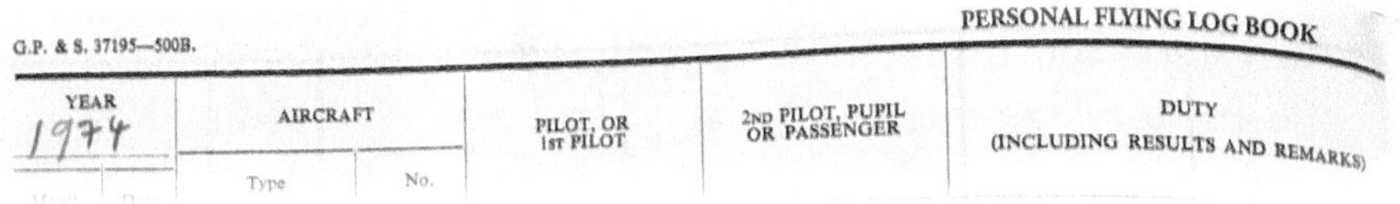
G.P. & S. 37195—500B.

PERSONAL FLYING LOG BOOK

YEAR	AIRCRAFT		PILOT, OR 1ST PILOT	2ND PILOT, PUPIL OR PASSENGER	DUTY (INCLUDING RESULTS AND REMARKS)
1974	Type	No.			

IN THE DARK

The young Duty flight lieutenant was becoming increasingly agitated. The sudden and unexpected arrival of two civilians from the secured area of the airport apron in the late afternoon had completely frazzled him. He had almost, literally, fallen off his chair when I had knocked on the glass panel of his office in the administration center.

After umpteen unsuccessful phone calls to establish the whereabouts of his OC, he had scrutinized a large manual, and then placed us under arrest. This

was after I had at first casually, then frantically and with escalating incredulity, tried without success to find the AIP addendum that emergency re-fuelling was authorized in spite of this being classified a restricted military airport.

However our arrest seemingly had not resolved his predicament. He was now in a dilemma_as to what to do with an arrested unhappy pilot, and his good-looking girlfriend with shapely long legs all the way up to her very short hot pants.

This provoked a frantic search for the CO. (Yes, this is when I also first learned that OC - Officer Commanding was up there, close to the Pope, and CO - Commanding Officer was the guy who actually had to boss people around, but was above everyone but the Officer Commanding.)

He eventually tracked the CO down in the bar at the Officers Mess, which shows how naïve the young lieutenant was, because if he had been a seasoned pilot, this is where he would have looked first.

As it turns out, so was the depot manager for the contracting fuel supplier, both apparently in a benign and benevolent mood at this late hour on a Sunday afternoon.

After a protracted series of "Yes Sir, Yes Sir, No Sir, I will Sir, Yes Sir," the lieutenant put down the phone and announced that the CO had authorized fuel, and that the fuel truck would be there shortly.

'Shortly' might have meant anything, but in this instance proved to be a remarkably quick twenty minutes or so. However even before the big 30,000 liter bowser had rounded the corner, the apron was suddenly infested with blue uniformed Air Force pilots of every rank, milling around the little Piper Colt like ants around a dead caterpillar.

Seemingly its arrival was a unique and extraordinary event, and the news had rapidly spread all over the base.

An initial seemingly insuperable crisis was overcome by pumping fuel into an empty dustbin, which had first been swilled out with several gallons of Avgas to clean it. This was after it became obvious that the giant nozzle and five inch diameter delivery pipe were not appropriate to haul up on top of a delicate fabric wing, with two inch filler holes.

There was no shortage of volunteers to man the little oscillating hand pump that had been found to now transfer the fuel from the dustbin to the top of the wing. Apparently every cadet wanted to claim his part in this memorable event.

All this while I was being peppered with every kind of inquiry: "How fast does this thing fly?" How high can it go? May I sit in it, Sir?"

Beginning to relax, while basking in the hub of all this attention and activity, my very recent trepidation was gradually being replaced by a calm conviction

that our arrest was now discounted, and I was not offended even when I overheard; "It's hard to believe that a little thing like this can actually fly."

It didn't take long for the tanks to fill flush with the filler caps, and none too soon, because by the time the Shell man had wound in his huge delivery pipe, the evening glow had dissolved to darkness, and night had set in.

Before he drove off, I had proffered the aircraft Carnet (fuel credit) card, but he was disinterested, said he had no means of processing it, and that I should settle it with the Airforce.

Most of the blue uniforms were beginning to drift back to the barracks and bar, and the Airforce was represented most noticeably by the young Duty lieutenant. I asked him how I should settle for the fuel, and at the same time, if I could use his phone to call my parents so that they could come and collect us. I pointed out that we would then depart early the next day as it was now obviously too dark for me to fly.

He looked at me in utter astonishment.

Did I not understand that the CO had authorized fuel only so that I should leave immediately after, and that he was to erase any record of my arrival in the incident log. This had simply never happened!

There was just absolutely no leeway for argument, and I found myself helping my girlfriend back into the cockpit, starting the motor, and making towards the taxiway on which we had arrived.

Brain numbed, I followed the broken white center-line, first glowing in the ambient light from the administration building, and then vaguely in the starlight. The moon was only a crescent sliver, but as my eyes became used to the darkness, the markings became more visible.

The guard at the taxiway gate had observed our return, and it was opened before we got there. The guard dog just sat on his haunches, and seemed to be grinning.

I was desperately trying to rationalize the situation we were in, whilst backtracking slowly down the runway center-line. The little Piper Colt was never adapted for night flying. No landing light, no navigation lights, no instrument lighting. There was a single panel light which was just enough for the luminous markings on the dials to visibly glow.

Did the Airforce not understand this? Did they not realize that I had no night rating, and only fifty five hours total logged flying time? I had tried to explain. They weren't listening.

I glanced at my completely oblivious girlfriend. She wore a smile, seemed to be glowing, and I realized that this was from all the attention she had been getting from the boys in blue. This would have help light the panel.

I turned 180° on the threshold numbers and preoccupied my stupefied focus on engine run-up and pre-flight checks, after which there was nothing left but to look out at the night. The diminutive crescent moon shone silver bright in the clear starlit dome above, giving way to the diffused light from the urban spread of the little town where I had been raised from my early teens.

I knew this town. I would find my way, and without further thought, pushed the throttle to the wall, abandoning our fate to fortune while tracking the vague center-line.

Leveling off at 1500 feet above ground revealed an obvious horizon, and I cast about to get my bearings. The street lights along the easily recognizable dual carriage main street would lead me out to the Bulawayo road, and my

departure airfield ran parallel to this, and between it and the industrial area.

I had gleaned from flying talk around the braai (barbecue) that in the event of an engine failure at night, the best option was to head for the biggest dark patch, plan an approach, trim for around stall speed plus 10 percent, and pray.

Positioned for final approach, with the tachometer set at 1,000 revs per minute, I cranked the trim handle anti-clockwise for an indicated airspeed of 65 miles per hour. Then selecting a spot on the windscreen a short distance up from the dashboard, I stared out at the dark patch. The spot on the windscreen appeared to be making steady progress for a point about one third of the length of the dark patch from its commencement. This was as good as it could be.

Tense and anxious, I stared ahead for some sign that would reveal the runway surface. The whitewashed markers had long assumed colour earth from neglect, and I was aware only that the blackness was now rapidly expanding to seemingly swallow us.

I know that I never attempted to flare, because the soft motion of the tyres trundling along the earthen runway took me completely by surprise. I didn't believe we were actually on the ground before we had rolled for perhaps 10 meters, and I clearly recall my astonishment.

I am still convinced that this is singularly the smoothest landing I have ever experienced, and wish that I could claim credit for its achievement. The outcome must be ascribed to the fact that I was newly qualified, and too stupid to understand the folly of it all. With a bit more experience I probably would have messed up totally.

I never did hear from the Airforce regarding the fuel. Clearly we had never been there.

To be alone in the air at night is to be very much alone. *Pauline Gower.*

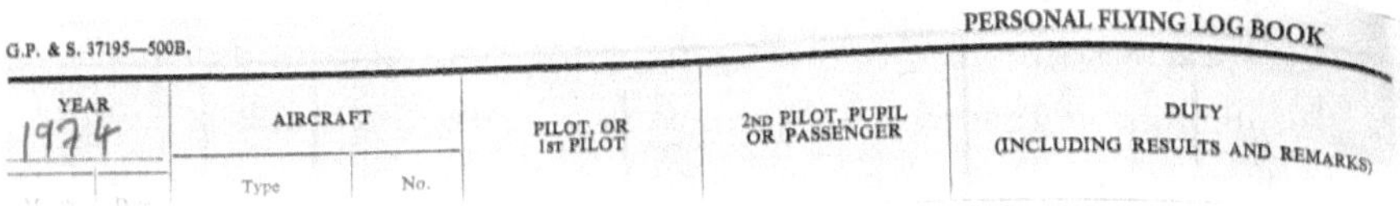
G.P. & S. 37195—500B.
PERSONAL FLYING LOG BOOK

YEAR	AIRCRAFT		PILOT, OR 1ST PILOT	2ND PILOT, PUPIL OR PASSENGER	DUTY (INCLUDING RESULTS AND REMARKS)
1974	Type	No.			

THE YANK

The summer climate in South Central Africa is almost exclusively influenced by the Inter Tropical Convergence Zone (ITCZ), and is characterised by thunderstorms of short duration when the rainfall can exceed one inch per hour. These generally occur mid, or late afternoon and are always followed by brilliant sunshine, sparkling the freshly washed earth. Requiring a forecast for more than the duration of the intended flight would probably have attracted some scepticism, and inevitably would have been "possible afternoon thundershowers".

It is a region where, except for the need to impress your friends, an instrument rating is redundant, and the weather almost entirely predictable.

However, there are instances (I've never bothered to find out why, perhaps the trade winds 'stall' or something), when following a general thunderstorm, it just carries on raining for as long as three weeks in one long deluge.

The odds for this might be just once in five years.

I remember one such occasion when Winco drove around his waterlogged tobacco crop, which was yellowed and wilting from root rot, with his hand out of the window waving a photograph of the sun. He hoped that this might encourage the plants to hang in there for better days. Eventually his Land Rover got bogged down and he'd had to walk home.

Justifiably Johnny never really gave serious thought to the weather when he flew off to visit his parents for the weekend with his wife, and he wasn't greatly worried when there was some general thunderstorm activity on Saturday afternoon.

It had dispersed by 14:30 and he made a mental note that this would easily allow him time to make the three hour trip home in daylight with the likelihood that this pattern would be repeated the following day. He anticipated the crisp rainbow-hued balm that would inevitably follow for a pleasant return flight.

By the Wednesday following the weekend, Johnny was desperate.

After the expected thunderstorm activity on Sunday, the clouds had (unpredictably) merely increased in density, and the steady downpour had continued unabated.

This was the early seventies, and the only alternative to flying was a 14-hour road trip via Salisbury, for which Johnny would have had to borrow a car. The railway passenger service took two days. Johnny just could not decide on whether to abandon the aircraft and find another way, or wait it out. He had been flying long enough to know the futility of phoning MET in the hope of an accurate and favourable prediction. His anxiety was intensified by the fact that he had only just been appointed as regional manager for a new corporate employer the previous month, and been at his new desk for less than ten days.

He was in big trouble.

His restless desperation had driven him to make his way up to the airfield every morning, always to be met with the same sight of his forlorn little Cherokee standing with its wheels almost totally immersed, barely visible through the cascade of water sheeting down the windscreen of his father's borrowed car, and the whole airfield looking like a rice paddy.

Today was different though. Firstly, the cloud cover was beginning to break, with small patches of blue between, and secondly, there was an old Aztec parked right alongside his Cherokee. The airfield, however was still covered in 4 inches of water.

"How the hell had that got here?" he thought. Despite his overriding anxiety, he was inquisitive enough to wade over for a closer inspection which revealed the leading edges of both of the Aztec's wings to be pock marked with indentations the size of the average fridge ice-tray. Johnny whistled with incredulity, wondering what extraordinary story this must tell.

He was then vaguely aware that what he might have previously mistaken for a gutter down pipe, had detached from under the overhang of a nearby hangar, and was laconically making its way towards him, wearing a leather jacket.

"Howdy," greeted the approaching stranger. Johnny wasn't able to respond without then immediately launching into an inquiry regarding the battered wings.

The stranger's reply was a wry smile, accompanied only by: "Yeah, we came through a couple big uns."

Johnny then felt provoked into an explanation of his desperate predicament.

He was aware that the Yank was looking at him speculatively before he responded; "I can tell you how you can get out of here if you do exactly as I say."

Johnny's desperate look invited the Yank to continue.

"Firstly, arrange your load so your center of gravity is as far back in the envelope as possible, and then pull the aircraft forward by hand before you start up. She will have subsided in the wet. Once she's fired up, get her really warm before you try and move; you're going to need a heap of power to get going. Follow the precise center of the taxi path, where the ground will be hardest from compaction. When you get to where you're sure the runway starts, you keep going until you have turned right around to face your best guess for the center-line."

"Now this is important," continued the Yank, "when you are sure of your center-line, pick a precise marker on the horizon. You're going to need this. Now wind her up for full power, allowing for the air being saturated, and pull the yoke right back against the stops so you have to suck your belly in. Right back! You must get that nose wheel outta the water before you've made a yard. No flaps. When she starts moving, the nose will be high and you won't see your marker, so you must keep her straight with the ball and DI. Now you get nimble on those pedals right off, you hear, getting away depends on it! There's going to be a lot of noise. This is the sound of water beating against the airframe, listen for it; it's going to tell you what you want to know. You ain't going to get much speed for a while, but relax, you ain't going to be using

runway either. When you hear the noise begin to fade, she will be starting to fly, and the main wheels will be coming up out of the water, so you can relax on the back pressure just a tad to lower the nose 'cause you're way on the wrong side of the drag curve. Soon you will suddenly feel her accelerate, and the noise will all but disappear. She's coming up on the plane. Wait for this, because now you can gently pull up one notch of flap, not before! Now lower the nose a tad more, and you keep those wings dead level and the prop hub pointed right at that marker. Think of nothing else and she'll just fly away out of ground effect all by herself."

Johnny felt his mouth go dry. He knew he had the skill, but was afraid of the challenge.

"I think I'll just try this now," he said, "It'll weigh less with just one up, and I won't be risking my wife's life, if I can get off ok, I'll go and fetch her."

"Sonny," the Yank responded, "I can tell you how you can take-off, but I sure as hell can't tell you how to land in this without going upside-down."

Half an hour later Johnny had returned with his wife, and was ready to go. There was no sign of the Yank.

Well, Johnny kept his cool, and it all turned out exactly as the Yank had said it would.

Johnny swears he was actually airborne in less than 300 yards, which must tell us something.

Three hours of flying later, and he was holding off above the welcoming tar of his hometown aerodrome. Lucky for Johnny, because it started to rain again during the night, and didn't let-up for another two weeks.

When I think about this, I have to wonder who that stranger might have been. Really lanky guy, Johnny had said, maybe six foot six. Looked a lot like Bob Hoover.

Luck has a quantum. There is a reservoir for this that can be filled with an intimate knowledge of your aeroplane, careful flight planning, a meticulous preflight, and acute situational awareness. If you can continually top this reservoir up, you will never run out of luck.

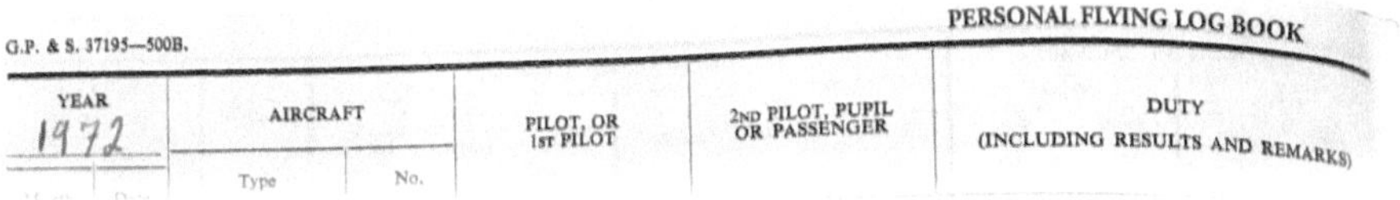
G.P. & S. 37195—500B.

PERSONAL FLYING LOG BOOK

YEAR	AIRCRAFT		PILOT, OR 1ST PILOT	2ND PILOT, PUPIL OR PASSENGER	DUTY (INCLUDING RESULTS AND REMARKS)
1972	Type	No.			

THE BASTARD

There were six of us sitting on the Clubhouse verandah behind cold beers, as was the custom on a Friday evening. Bob was bitterly relating how he had failed his initial PPL flight test, that very day.

Not that he had a chance in hell of passing.

Everybody knew that the Senior Civil Aviation Flight-Test Inspector never, ever passed anyone on his or her first attempt, but nevertheless insisted on taking every initial test.

They said that this had been his steadfast practice since his appointment in the late '50s.

There were some that said he did it purposely, to impress upon the would-be pilot that nothing came easy, and persistence was required to be really competent. They reckoned that this was why we could boast one of the best safety records of any country in the Commonwealth.

Then there were others who said that it was because he didn't have the courage to take the responsibility if someone he passed then pranged. He left the burden for this to one of the junior flight testers. They said the safety record was due entirely to our wonderful weather.

Then again, there were those that reckoned he just did it out of malice.

We had all heard how he was supposed to have suffered some dreadful experience involving fire during the war, which is why he always wore welding gloves and a padded jacket, and perhaps this could be a factor.

"Did you hear what happened to Chuck?" asked James, "apparently, while they were walking out to the aircraft, the bastard asked him what he thought "that cloud was doing up there," obviously expecting a meteorological analysis. Chuck thought he would crack a witty to ease the tension, and suggested that "maybe it had come up for the weekend". The Bastard stopped mid-stride, told Chuck he had failed, just like that, and walked back to the clubhouse."

"But I thought I had a chance," protested Bob, "and I was determined to be the only one in the country ever to have passed on his first attempt since 1960."

If anyone could have done it, it would probably have been Bob. He showed special aptitude right from the start, went solo after only 5 hours, had accumulated a total of 57 hours before being able to confirm his test booking, and had scored over 90% in all the written papers.

Bob's appointment had been for 9am, but there had been no sign of the Senior Flight Inspector by 10:30, and becoming a bit rattled, Bob had phoned the DCA offices to find out whether perhaps he might have been forgotten.

"He is conducting a flight test," was the response.

He confided his growing anxiety to a passing pilot, who laughed, and explained that he did this to all his victims, to get them thoroughly flustered.

Bob began to feel his anxiety being replaced by cold anger.

By the time the Flight-Tester finally arrived, just after twelve, Bob says he had been drained of all emotion, except controlled fury, and reduced to a dispassionate machine with steely determination.

He reckons the whole test was executed with textbook precision, in spite of every trick being thrown at him, and the throttle being pulled on three occasions for demonstration of a forced landing. For each he had responded with reflex precision, articulating all his actions aloud in a terse clipped tone, whilst smoothly progressing from one to the next, speed to height, trim for glide, direction wind, find field, establish pattern, find fault, warn pax, mayday call, master and fuel off, call marker, demonstrate safe execution on the nail, and then smooth positive recovery.

After they had landed, the inspector seemed to have changed his whole demeanour, and in the friendliest way suggested they de-brief over a spot of lunch, during which Bob parried questions about gyroscopic and asymmetric blade effect, Differential and Friez ailerons, Fowler flaps, methods for reducing the effect of wing tip vortices and preventing control flutter, trim systems for stabilators and elevators, horn balance, angles for incidence and washout (a lot of which was not appropriate for the type of aircraft in which the test had been conducted), and on, and on.........

Bob knew his stuff, and slowly began to feel a lightening of spirit, developing into giddy elation when it seemed that there was nothing on which he could be tripped up. His heart began to sing, He was actually going to make it!

Finally, after draining his coffee and dabbing his lips with a napkin, the Flight –Tester stood up, and brusquely announced.

"I'm sorry, but you've failed."

In spite of his best intentions to remain calm, Bob blurted "But why?"

"I am not obliged to divulge that, but you may apply for your Test Result Sheet on payment of the relevant fee," he responded, and walked away, abandoning Bob to pay for the lunch.

The BASTARD!

We laughed. This was just another of his well-known tricks.

"He must have earned some respect though," proffered Paul, "they say that almost every person in the flying fraternity pitched up for his funeral."

"Yea," countered John, "but they say that was just to make sure there was no chance he was ever coming back."

It is a good thing to learn caution from the misfortunes of others.

Publilius Syrus

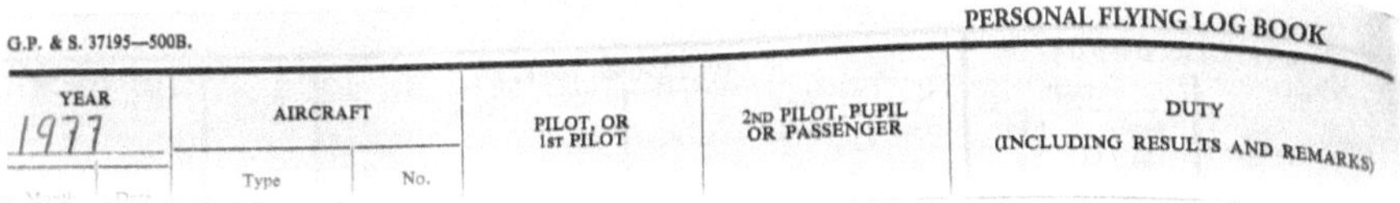
G.P. & S. 37195—500B.

PERSONAL FLYING LOG BOOK

YEAR	AIRCRAFT		PILOT, OR 1ST PILOT	2ND PILOT, PUPIL OR PASSENGER	DUTY (INCLUDING RESULTS AND REMARKS)
1977	Type	No.			

STALL WARNING

The only time I wasn't fixated on the stall warning light was when the sweat from my forehead trickled into my eyes, and I had to squeeze them tight and wipe them with a fistful of T-shirt to ease the intense stinging.

The ominous glow of that red orb wasn't just flickering on; it was more like occasionally flickering off! Sometimes it seemed to just glow malevolently.

"Definitely buffalo" mumbled Sarel.

Screw the fucking Buffalo, I wanted to scream, look at the fucking stall-warning light!

We were around 300 feet above ground level, with 1800 rpm set, and endlessly orbiting left at about 30 degrees of bank so that Sarel could peer at the bush below, looking for signs of movement in the Zambezi valley.

It was the first time I had ever flown with Sarel after being appointed his 'observer', and I suppose the only thing that stopped me from screaming was the fact that he had such a reputation. He was an old hand at this, and I was the rookie. Then of course, these were dangerous times anyway, and spinning in was just one of the options. If it was your day, it was your day. It wasn't a time when you might consider giving up smoking for your health.

Later, perhaps on the fifth or sixth occasion that I flew with Sarel, I began to relax enough to observe him. Whilst he was intently looking out of his window, he never once looked at the airspeed, and there was constant gentle co-ordinated movement between yoke and rudder, with the pitch held on the right side of the power curve. Even before there was the slightest suggestion of a wing drop, Sarel would almost imperceptibly push the yoke forward to decrease the angle of attack, combined with gentle opposite rudder, just enough to lift the wayward wing, all the while staring down at the bush below.

Even when we were working between the cliff faces in one of the escarpment ravines, with topographical gusts coming from nowhere, and unexpected thermals bouncing up off superheated rocks, he never looked away from his constant reading of the signs on the ground. The worst it got was the tell-tale juddering just before a full-on-stall, at which point Sarel would casually jam the piece of cold cooked boerewors (South African farm sausage) on which he was always chewing between his teeth, in order to free his right hand, so he could apply a tad more power to recover the lost height.

Sarel was not an articulate person, and if you asked him about his flying technique, he would become perplexed and look at you blankly. It wouldn't occur to him that he might be pushing the envelope way over the limit. He was just doing the job the best way he knew.

But then he expected nothing less from anyone else, and when he asked that I fly from the right seat so that he could get a bead on his target below, he was always yelling at me to "tighten up, and keep the bloody wing down!"

It didn't help that the wire contraption with the hessian bag that he had rigged up to catch the empty cartridge cases never worked, no matter how many times he re-designed it, assuring me on each occasion that he had "got it right this time".

The burning hot shells from the RPD that he had mounted through the Cherokee 180 pilot's storm window would bounce around the cockpit from all directions, and inevitably down the back of my shirt, or nestle in my crotch.

It was hard enough just to focus on best positioning the aircraft for Sarel, while monitoring the height and airspeed without having to contend with this stinging onslaught, combined with a fog of cordite and the hideous noise in that confined space.

If you couldn't animate Sarel with hangar talk, you could certainly get him going if you invited an explanation as to his engineering ingenuity regarding his mounted RPD (Kalashnikov light machine gun).

He had replaced the butt with hand grips on each side of the breech and devised a swivel mounting, to which he had rigged stops in the form of geometric curves to prevent him from shooting off the wing leading edge on the one hand, and the prop tips on the other, and there was a complicated feeder system to prevent the ammunition belt from tangling in the control yolk. It was a point of constant aggravation for Sarel that the Cessna jockeys were able to mount all sorts of arsenal to the floors of their 'planes, which they could then fly with the doors off. There was even a Cessna 172 with a four barreled Browning mounted on a tripod in the Police Reserve Air-wing fleet.

Sarel was just one of a number of a small band in the Air-wing who had learned to read tracks from the air with incredible accuracy, and could not only identify the type of animal that had caused them, but even how fresh or stale they were. Acutely tuned in to every hint; the different colour pebbles presented for the time that they had been dislodged, how the long grass was bending, the amplitude of its curves, and the form of the swathe that cut through it. All of this from an optimum of 300 to 500 ft above ground, depending on the time of day, and how the light was slanting.

I wished I could fly like Sarel intuitively aware of every hint of roll, each nuance of yaw.

I have never come even close, because I have never been able to afford the hours it would take. In the end, that level of proficiency can only be attained from endless practice of flying 'on the edge', and the only people with that sort of opportunity are the likes of aerobatic pilots, crop sprayers and police, military or rescue pilots.

The rest of us just have to do the best we can.

I do this as much as possible vicariously. Every time I read of a light aircraft crash, I try to figure out the reason, and decide what I might have done in the same circumstances.

I read everything related to flying experiences that I can lay my hands on, and imagine myself in every kind of situation. Only this way can I hope to avoid that damning epitaph, "pilot error".

It is as hard for me to imagine that Sarel might become the victim of a light aircraft accident, as it would for Bob Hoover.

I bumped into Sarel about two years ago, more than twenty years after the last time we flew together. We caught up a bit on the intervening years, and after a time I asked him if he was still flying. He told me he had let his licence lapse about five years before, after having to leave his farm for a small-holding just outside town.

I suppose there was no longer good enough reason for him continue to fly. What an incredible waste of a colossal talent.

But if I had suggested this to Sarel, he would have just looked at me blankly. Perplexed.

Always plan for several options. Always keep one option spare.

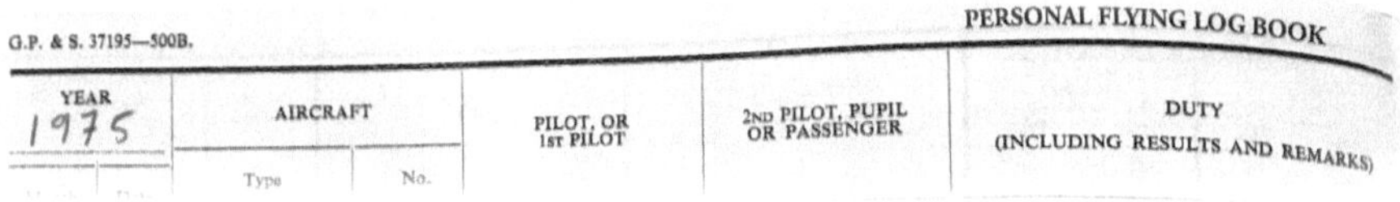
G.P. & S. 37195—500B.
PERSONAL FLYING LOG BOOK

YEAR 1975	AIRCRAFT		PILOT, OR 1ST PILOT	2ND PILOT, PUPIL OR PASSENGER	DUTY (INCLUDING RESULTS AND REMARKS)
	Type	No.			

MARK HIM ABSENT

They say that it was the biggest collection of crop sprayers gathered in one place. Ever.

They had been summonsed from everywhere in the region, even from as far north as Kenya, but the biggest contingents by far were from Zimbabwe and South Africa. The cause for all this aerial activity was some pestilence that had manifested itself in the sugar cane on the Pungwe flats in Mozambique.

The nature of this thing was that, if allowed to spread, it would quickly become uncontrollable, and would wipe out the whole Mozambican sugar industry. After which, it could just as easily find its way down the coast into Natal where virtually the whole of South Africa's sugar production subsists. To add to the element of urgency, it had to be eliminated within a specific time period to interrupt the cycle, otherwise it might re-appear, and spread, rendering the whole immensely expensive crop spraying exercise to have been fruitless. It must have been like rust in wheat, with the ability to spread like wildfire. Then again, it might even have been "wildfire", which is a name given to a particular fungal disease found in tobacco crops. However, deliberating the type and potency of this disease is irrelevant to the point of this story.

When Ian received his orders, he packed his little duffel bag, and told his long time loyal assistant Timoti Mashangu to do the same. They then loaded the bulk material container in front of the cockpit (called the hopper) with as many cans of fuel as it would take, leaving just enough room for Timoti, made as comfortable as possible on top of the blanket rolls, and they were off.

Crop sprayers are not made for endurance over long distances, and their whole load potential is dedicated to the hopper content, with little allowance for fuel which is only required for as long as it takes to disperse the load. Ian had to travel a respectable distance, and in order to accomplish this, he would wait until his fuel was down to about a quarter, find a suitable open patch so that he could land, and then, with the help of Timoti, top up from the cans in his hopper.

In due time, even in the coastal haze, Ian was able to discern the airfield ahead, with glints of white and yellow, representing acres of aircraft, and as he drew closer, began to recognise the markings of some of his colleagues and cronies.

Temporarily overcome with the excitement of this extraordinary panorama, and aware that his approach would be being observed, he pushed the nose down for a near maximum red-line speed dive, screaming low and level down the runway, and then pulling the nose up into a graceful 2 G parabola. Glancing at the horizon on each side, he kept the wing trailing edges equidistant from the horizon line with rudder. After passing vertical Ian eased off the back

pressure on the stick to keep the loop round whilst gradually adding power.

He was suddenly brought to his senses by the sight of Timoti's legs, as well as a number of other paraphernalia exiting the hopper. Yanking the stick back to re-establish some positive G, he was able to scoop Timoti back in, and landed without further ado.

As soon as the crop sprayer came to a standstill, Timoti leapt from the hopper in one mighty bound, only briefly pausing white faced (ok, a sort of shade of yellow then), to look around in abject terror, before running headlong into the sugar cane.

He didn't reappear, and I hope those M'Senas and Machicundas were hospitable towards him as he made his way back to Zimbabwe through the bush, because whilst he was from the eastern districts, he wasn't even a Makaranga. He was actually a Makorekore, but they are an affiliate tribe, belonging to the generic Masezuru who all speak dialects of the mother Mashona tongue.

If a pilot chooses to indulge in a moment of sudden spontaneous exuberance, the consequence for this folly should be his alone.

G.P. & S. 37195—500B. PERSONAL FLYING LOG BOOK

YEAR	AIRCRAFT		PILOT, OR 1ST PILOT	2ND PILOT, PUPIL OR PASSENGER	DUTY (INCLUDING RESULTS AND REMARKS)
1998	Type	No.			

THE VERY TALENTED AIR TRAFFIC CONTROLLER

"Quelimane tower, Echo Lima Bravo, showing eight nautical miles GPS from the South East, please may we have your joining and landing."

"Echo Lima Bravo, you are cleared to one thousand feet, call left base runway 36, QNH 1018, wind light and variable."

"Thank you sir, kindly confirm you were notified requirement for customs and fuel uplift?"

"Affirmative, personnel are available at your disposal."

It sounded good, and it's great when a plan comes together with everything working out predictably.

We were from Lanseria outside Johannesburg, and had managed to find fuel in transit at Buffalo Range in Zimbabwe. It was a relief that we might now be able to expedite immigration and re-fuelling in good time for our final leg to Angoche, another hour and a half north.

It was already 15:00hrs local time.

The sun sets early in August on the east coast and it can be suddenly dark as early as 17:30 at this time of year, added to which there is always a very strong possibility of sea mist along the coastline. Angoche airfield is a 1,000m strip of red dirt in the middle of a palm forest, with a frond-thatched hut off one side. It would be impossible to find it in the dark, and that would leave no alternative but to return to Quelimane.

It was also going to be an advantage that we had amongst us as a passenger, the person of Angelo, who had been born in Lorenzo Marques and could speak fluent Portuguese. He knew the ropes.

Well after landing, there was a lot of gesticulation and argument before it was all settled at US$ 100.00 (about ZAR 800.00 at the time). Angelo beamed his pride, explaining that he had negotiated this all inclusive of Landing Fees, Approach Fees, Navigation Fees, Parking Fees as well as Departure Fees.

We were a bit dubious as to the result of these negotiations however, and felt that the list of 'fees' might have exceeded the official standard, but what the hell, we were running out of time, and who was going to split hairs when there was some urgency.

Certainly not worth arguing that the approach and navigation fees were superfluous, since both the NDB* and VOR* transmitters had not been working for some years. (* Radio aids for navigation.)

Of course passenger tax and transit fees were extra, and the final tally was considerably higher than experienced at either Lanseria or Buffalo Range en-route.

We bundled back into the 'plane, and fired up.

"QuelimaneTower, Echo Lima Bravo?"................................No reply.

"Quelimane Tower, Echo Lima Bravo?"................................No reply.

"Quelimane Tower, Echo Lima Bravo?"

Seven more attempts!..................Still no reply!

Eventually, ... "Last caller, Quelimane Tower, I have your carrier wave, but no voice."

That's funny; everything was working perfectly inbound!

Switch radios, and try again. Same result!

"Last caller, this is Quelimane Tower, I have your carrier wave, but no voice."

This is bizarre. There must be some electro-magnetic field blocking transmission. We could see the little controller sitting in his tower, looking down at us.

Maybe if we moved the aircraft a bit, for a better signal position?

Immediately the radio crackled into life, loudly proclaiming "Echo Lima Bravo, this is an International airport; no movement is permitted on the apron or aerodrome, without prior clearance in accordance with international law!"

Nothing else for it, we would have to close down and go and speak to the man.

Hopefully we could appeal to his better nature and ask him to exercise some latitude, and allow us to depart non-radio. They were working perfectly inbound, and would probably come back on line as soon as we were airborne. Impossible that both radios had failed simultaneously!

Back inside the building, the girl at the counter inscrutably pointed out a red 'phone at one end, and soon after picking it up, I had the man in the tower on the other end.

My plea for some leniency fell on deaf ears, and he insisted that I must seek the services of a 'radio tekneeshun'. When I asked him how this might be possible at nearly 4pm on a Friday afternoon, he offered to try his best to find just such a person for us, though he conceded that this might be very difficult at such short notice.

I wandered disconsolately back to the aircraft, and after explaining our predicament to the passengers, was then overjoyed to see a man in blue overalls walking briskly towards us, tool box in hand.

Within seconds he had the whole radio stack in his lap, which prompted the thought that this might be a very useful talent should he be in the practice of relieving cars of their radios at the local shopping center parking lot.

Angelo remarked that he bore an uncanny resemblance to the licensing official to whom he had paid the landing and other fees, just only now in a blue overall, instead of a blue shirt and peaked cap. Perhaps a close relative?

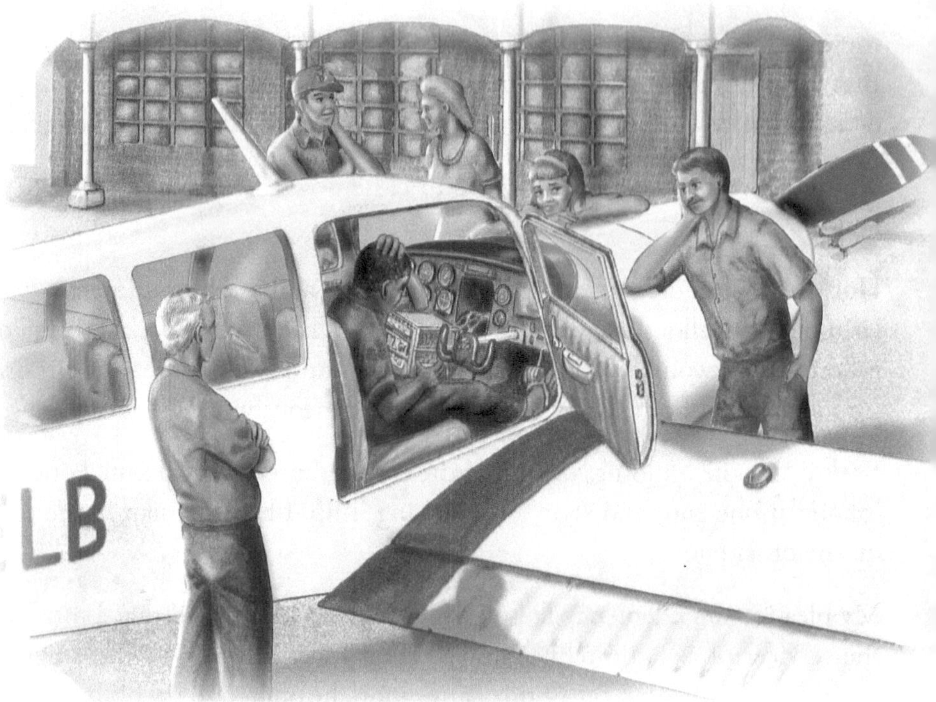

After he had put the radios back in position, he donned my headset and asked me "where was the master switch?" so he could test them.

Incredibly everything seemed to be in working order again when he spoke to the tower, and I asked him how much?

He pulled a tatty invoice book from his pocket, and wrote out an invoice for, wait for it, ZAR.800.00.

We paid him, and wasted no time boarding for fastest possible departure.

"Quelimane Tower, Echo Lima Bravo?"................................ No reply.

"Quelimane Tower, Echo Lima Bravo?" Three more times......Still no reply!

Dear God, please, not again.

Suddenly. “Echo Lima Bravo, Quelimane Tower, proceed to holding point 36, and advise when ready for ATC.”

Funny, the man was panting, obviously out of breath.

Out of breath? From running up the tower steps?

Stunned at how badly we had been conned, we nevertheless knew we had no option but to comply with procedures to get out of that place, or run the risk of new reasons for delay.

It was at least an hour later, after skimming along at 500 feet above the endless white sands bordered by waving palms on the one side, and soporific rolling waves on the other, that I could calm down sufficiently so as to come to terms with our fleecing.

Challenge him on return? Did he not realise that he would discourage the potential for tourism if this was how he behaved?

No, in Africa, the promise of tomorrow is better if it can be made the certainty of today.

Surely even a fool could understand the wisdom of this logic.

There is one thing that is common to both pilots and air traffic controllers. This is that if the pilot errs, the pilot and his passengers will suffer the consequences, and if the air traffic controller errs, the pilot and his passengers will suffer the consequences.

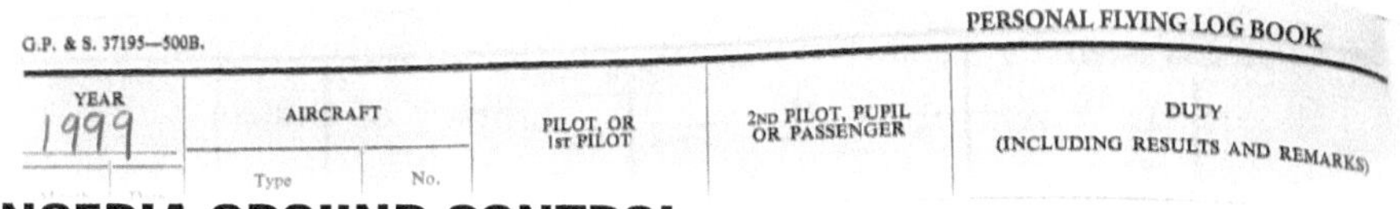
G.P. & S. 37195—500B.

PERSONAL FLYING LOG BOOK

YEAR	AIRCRAFT		PILOT, OR 1ST PILOT	2ND PILOT, PUPIL OR PASSENGER	DUTY (INCLUDING RESULTS AND REMARKS)
1999	Type	No.			

LANSERIA GROUND CONTROL

One of the things truly comforting about flying, is that all traffic control procedures and protocols are precisely defined by rules. There are internationally prescribed flight levels based on Visual Flight rules, or Instrument flight rules, depending on the magnetic heading, to ensure vertical separation. There are standard approach procedures, and standard departure procedures for high traffic-density airports. There are imperative procedures for approach and joining the circuit for, and departure from, an unmanned airfield.

For every eventuality, there is a contingent rule. If there is a loss of electrical power and failure of avionics in flight, there is a precise procedure which must be followed, and all involved will understand what to expect for safe conduct and conclusion of the flight. Breach of any of these rules is always transparent. Even whilst taxiing on the ground, there are decreed rights of way. What can possibly go wrong? Collision is theoretically impossible.

This is unlike road traffic rules, which are pretty much open to personal interpretation, and breach of which are only accountable after the transgressor has, perchance, been ambushed by one means or another for official processing.

From its very birthing, despite the sometimes steeply undulating slopes on the terminal apron and taxiways, the dream that Lanseria Airport would become the second most important aviation hub, servicing Johannesburg and central South Africa, was rapidly becoming a reality.

Either good publicity, or otherwise kind fate, ordained that just one year after the airport was opened, it was chosen to host Air Africa International in

1975, a major event originally contrived for Farnborough and Paris. This was then followed by air shows with international participation in 1977, 1979, and 1981. Perhaps this influenced the support of the then Department of Transport who, just three years after it was established, declared that Lanseria should become the new terminal for all visiting aircraft from foreign countries, in spite of it being privately owned.

It was becoming the obvious base of choice for privately owned executive jets, and small commercial operators. For a while, even the air force established a presence, and subsequently in the late nineties, a number of regional airlines began to operate from there.

In spite of all this growing eminence and increase in traffic, during my frequent acquaintance with Lanseria for renewal of my license or other training in the mid 1990's, all movement on the airport apron and taxiways was regulated through the tower frequency, and informal jocular banter could often be heard between the tower and a number of the pilots and flight school instructors who had made it their base. The airport atmosphere was both efficient and friendly.

Then, just after the onset of the new millennium the South African Government decided to review the grading of all airports, and Lanseria was declared the only one privately owned that was to retain its international status. This was otherwise only accorded to the nine Government controlled airports servicing the major provincial cities.

Previously, passport control had been available at a number of smaller airports, and I hadn't had cause to fly into Lanseria for perhaps the past two years. Now it became the only gateway to neighbouring Botswana and Namibia.

This of course required that Lanseria go through yet another major upgrade to both its terminal facilities and runways in order to accommodate the ever increasing demand for its services.

I needed to fly to Gaberone.

Knowing that there were extensive alterations in progress and that one of the runways was closed, my bush pilot temperament predisposed me to feeling a little anxious as to what I might expect, and I hoped that there would be no potential for my knowledge of procedures and practices in a very busy International circuit being unpredictably tested.

In spite of having filed a flight plan some hours before, after declaring the field in sight, I was instructed to orbit my current position and maintain altitude until further instruction. Listening to prioritized flights being slotted in for final approach and landing, I was pleasantly surprised when after only fifteen minutes I was instructed to join right hand downwind for runway 06 left.

After an impeccable touch down, just after the threshold at stall speed, I was told I must; "Exit taxiway Lima".

I was aware I had just crossed a taxiway intersection, but did not see any designator.

The runway looked mighty long.

"ELB, repeat runway exit instruction!" Terse.

My hand reflexively pushing the throttle lever forward, I needed to find the 'L', and exit expeditiously! "Er, ELB exit taxi Lima". I responded and my ears began to feel warm in anticipation of the potential for embarrassment.

Another intersection appeared, but my straining eyes did not detect the sought for 'L'. Now past, I pondered that that might have been it?

Aware that there was a Cessna 208 in the circuit not far behind me, and knowing that he must by now have turned final, but was prohibited from making the call until I was clear of the runway, exacerbated my anxiety. I didn't want to be seen conspicuously as the reason for provoking a go around in such congested traffic.

Near V1(take-off speed) now with a strong possibility that I might become airborne, I saw yet another taxiway appearing to the left, together with the 24 runway threshold numbers not far beyond. No 'L', but this had to be it! I pulled back the power lever applying heavy braking, and turned left on to the taxiway.

Immediately I heard the Cessna call "final", get clearance to land, and I was told to contact 'ground control' on 121 decimal 65.

'Ground control'? Was this new?

Ground control asked me where I wished to go, and I was instructed to make turns at designators that were not there, to stop before and proceed after, and wished I had paid more attention to the last batch of NOTAMs (official periodic notices to airmen). The signs were not yet in place, but everyone else seemed to know where to go. I knew where Customs and Immigration was located, and intelligent tracking of the painted lines got me in front of the right place without humiliation; and then I am told to contact 'Parking' on 122 decimal 85.

Parking? This was definitely new. Obviously the explosive expansion required more exacting airport controls and regulation.

I made the call, was directed to follow a small orange truck with a flashing orange light on the roof, and was led to a series of white painted markings on the tar, then instructed to park in bay 'Alpha One'.

There was no lettering indicating bay 'Alpha One'. I protested this to the parking controller, and asked him where I needed to go. He jumped out of his truck, and used his dayglow orange batons to guide me into position. He then told me I must "Shut down my engine, and apply my parking brake".

My sensitivity now challenged, I wondered did he perceive me as an idiot? Did I sound indecisive or perhaps querulous over the radio? Of course I was going to shut down my engine, and apply my parking brake! Would I leave the engine running with the park brake off? Did he think I needed his instruction as to how I should operate an aeroplane? Was he perhaps being facetious?

Suddenly Dave, my passenger in the right hand seat, wrenched open the door with a yell, while pointing frantically at the parking controller's truck, now quickly gaining momentum towards a parked King Air. We were presented with the spectacle of his frantic efforts for opening the door of his rapidly accelerating truck at a full run, and he only just managed to stop his vehicle before it collided with the King Air's left wheel strut. It would have been comical if the anticipated consequence wasn't so dire.

Back in the aeroplane after completing immigration and customs formalities, and only after switching on the radio again, did I learn that he issued this same instruction to all arriving aircraft. Perhaps it is an ICAO (International Civil Aviation Organization) edict for parking procedure at international airports? I had never heard it before.

In any event Mister Parking Controller, when you stop your vehicle, you must, **"Shut down your engine and apply your parking brake."**

The best safety device is the pilot, who, deep down, regardless of the aircraft, retains a sense of fallibility, and vulnerability. No system can ever replace that.

Arnold Reiner

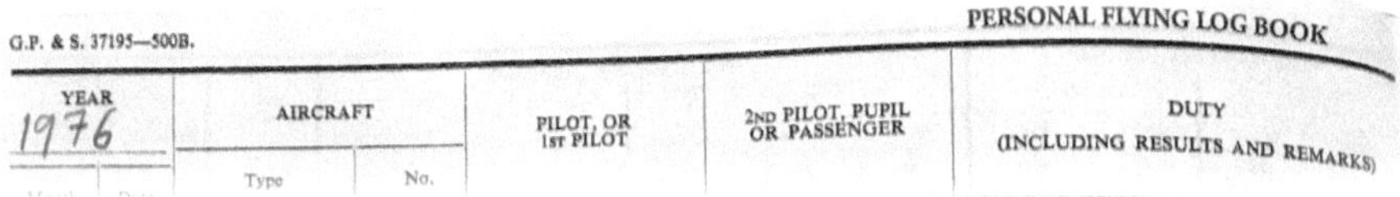

DOWN ON THE FARM

After Len 'phoned to tell his city friend Bob that he had finally put the finishing touches to his new farm strip, Bob wasted no time making an arrangement to fly out for the weekend. It would be an exciting break for his two children, and the wives being old school pals would be delighted at the opportunity for spending some time with each other again.

More importantly for Bob, it was an excuse to fly somewhere in his recently acquired 182, which was of course his obsessive pride and joy.

Everyone's keen anticipation was finally fulfilled after a 45-minute flight, and Bob had greased it on, having first sedately buzzed his old friend already eagerly waiting at the new strip.

Bob carefully tied down his pride and joy, and after a final look to make absolutely sure all was secure, he clambered into the Double-cab beside Len. The others were already in place, with ten-year-old Tommy and eight year old Lisa excitedly sitting in the open back.

After a short distance beyond a grove of Camel-thorn trees, they came to an open gate, and when the Double-cab came to a halt, little Tommy leapt out to close it, keen to demonstrate his initiative, and wanting to show that townees knew about these things, and could be helpful to have around.

He quickly swung the gate around to the hitching post, but was then perplexed by the fact that there was apparently no way of fastening it.

Well, we all know how those farmers have a reputation for 'making a plan', and there is no place they like to demonstrate this more than with the variety,

and ingenuity they apply to fastening a farm gate, lest we might forget just how clever they can be.

This one had an oval ring welded vertically, with a short section of piping serving as a sleeve. If you are familiar with this arrangement, you will lift the sleeve, which will then reveal a slot cut in the oval, through which you can now insert the last link of the short section of chain attached to the gate, and then allow the sleeve to drop down again, locking the chain in place.

Even the cleverest cow would not be able to work this out.

Little Tommy just saw an oval ring on the post, and a section of chain attached to the gate, with no way of fastening it.

He glanced around at the truck, feeling his ears begin to burn with embarrassment at the thought of having to ask for help, but the adults were all animatedly talking. Tommy yanked the piece of chain in the hope of miraculously stretching it so as wrap through the oval ring. No luck. For Tommy time seemed to stretch interminably while he tried to find a solution. Eventually he was able to carefully balance the last two links wedged over the top of the ring, making it look as if it had been fastened. He then scuttled back to the double-cab.

A lot of Saturday was spent going around the farm, with Len proudly showing off his various agricultural endeavours.

One of the highlights had been watching the cattle being fed from of the back of a one-ton pick-up. As soon as the truck entered the paddock, the cattle had started a stampede towards it from every direction, amassing around a much-trampled spot where it first stopped to deposit a pile of concentrate. By this time the pick-up had moved on, and those cattle that had been unable to shoulder their way into the feeding morass, had taken off after it again at a gallop, gamboling and frolicking with tails held high, and mooing for all they were worth.

This was repeated at about ten regular spots, by which time the herd had thinned considerably, and the pick-up was able to make its escape back through the gate.

All of this greatly amused the watchers, and prompted Bob to ask Len what might happen if the cattle actually caught up with the pick-up.

"They'd butt and nudge it, and have the side mirrors off in a blink", answered Len. "They get quite destructive. If you've ever bottle-fed a calf, you'll know how violently they nudge their noses into the bottle. This is supposed to stimulate the mother's udder, and encourage milk production. How the mother isn't permanently damaged is a wonder". He continued, "After being weaned, they're conditioned into substituting the pick-up for mother, and will persistently lick, butt, and push against it in the hope of satiating their hunger."

Sunday morning was spent fishing down on the farm dam, and there was a general feeling of increasing melancholy with the thought that the time for going home was drawing near. Except for Bob, who was secretly looking forward to getting behind the controls again.

Nearing the airstrip, they were horrified to discover that the gate had somehow been pushed wide open, with a swathe of cattle spoor pock marking the track between the posts.

His heart beginning to race, Bob was overcome with a dreadful foreboding for the spectacle that might be awaiting them.

His worst fears were realized as they rounded the last of the Masasa trees. Where his aircraft had been parked was a vast milling conglomerate of prime

beef, with just the top of the fin protruding in the center. While the occupants of the double-cab stared in horror, the first of the nearest steers began their gallop towards the newly arrived mother.

Prepare for the unknown, unexpected and inconceivable. After 50 years of flying I am still learning every time I fly.

Gene Cernan

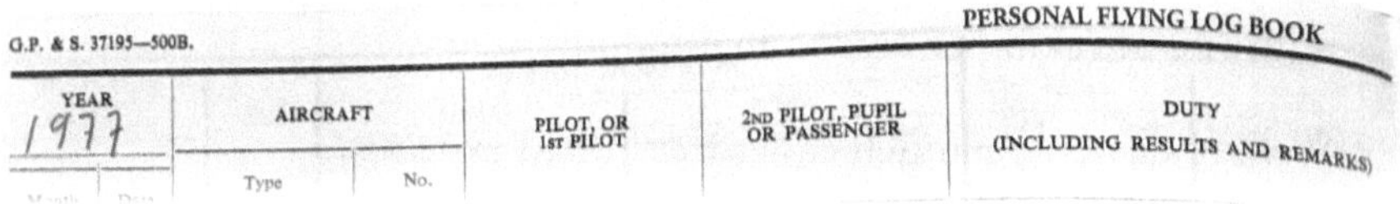
G.P. & S. 37195—500B.

PERSONAL FLYING LOG BOOK

YEAR	AIRCRAFT		PILOT, OR 1st PILOT	2nd PILOT, PUPIL OR PASSENGER	DUTY (INCLUDING RESULTS AND REMARKS)
1977	Type	No.			

CITABRIA DOWN

Log book entry, 16th Feb 1977, **Type**; Citabria, **Number**; VP-YYX, **Duty**; Conversion Flight Test, Result – crashed.

That's it; the log book entry; – "crashed" - without even a capital "C"?

It just doesn't cut it! It doesn't even start to describe the night sweats from shame and humiliation that haunted me for years following that sorry event.

We were all in our late twenties, (or at most a year or two over thirty), and all settler farmers with abundant access to Agricultural Assistance Board funds (for financing our crops), sitting on top of a koppie on military observation duty as part of our defense programme.

With such an opportune captive audience, I had subtly broached the subject of flying, and was gratified to hear the hoped for responses of; "I've always wanted to learn to fly", and "me too", followed of course, by the uninformed observations of; "too expensive" and "no time".

This was my cue. I was eager to argue that we could buy a suitable trainer for as little as $7,000-00, with which I could then teach them to fly from the local village airstrip. I confidently asserted that we would easily be able to obtain the services of a supervisory full instructor, who would only be required to make occasional visits to check compliance to regulations, and sign off first solos and cross country. I indicated that we could always fly and collect him for the day, when required.

Understand that I had qualified as an Assistant Instructor some nine months before, was in possession of this hard earned rating, but had no one to instruct, and time was running out. Regulations required logging a minimum of 25 hours instruction per year to maintain currency.

Well, it all went so much easier than I had expected.

In no time I had six enthusiastic participants, and within just weeks I was sitting waiting for Paul to convert me on to the Citabria that the seven of us had bought for just $1,000-00 each. (Mine out of the Agricultural Assistance Board budget for 'unanticipated contingencies', with the notated explanation:'casual labour required for removing rocks.')

Paul kept me waiting, and I had nothing better to do than read the Citabria manual, which is a little ambiguous regarding loading, and I was left with the impression that you had a choice between two up, and full tanks, but not both.

The tanks were full.

It was late evening and it had begun to drizzle, though the cloud layer was high and the light good.

Paul arrived with this sort of vacant look and inane grin, which supported the rumours that he hadn't been going home directly to his wife after work for a couple of months now, and he was impatient with my elementary questions.

To add to my woes, at the threshold, full static rpm yielded only 2,150, but should not have been less than 2,250 (according to the manual). After query, Paul yelled from behind me that he had flown the aircraft the day before, and it was fine. So we were now roaring down the runway like an edge trimmer, and had the ASI (air speed indicator) tremulously pointing at about 60 mph, when I eased back on the stick. There was a vague rising, accompanied by a lot of buffeting, before we sank back down on to the tar, now only indicating 55.

"I'm going to abort," I yelled to Paul. "Just hold the nose down," he yelled back, so I did, (he was the senior instructor) and we were now nearly out of usable runway, so I waited for 70, and this time easing the stick back resulted in perhaps thirty feet altitude, and a return to 60 mph airspeed. I pushed the stick forward ever so slightly again, which slowly allowed the speed to increase, but wasn't doing much for altitude.

Trouble was, a line of trees loomed, and I had no choice but to ease the stick back to clear these, as a consequence of which we were quickly back down to 60 again.

Over the top, gently ease over towards the biggest open space with minimal input of stick and rudder, stick forward, note airspeed creeping up, judge best distance from next obstacle for slight stick-back to clear it, over the top, dry swallow, wipe palms on trousers so stick not so slippery, gently point to the biggest open space with minimal input…..and repeat.

This went on for about three miles, during which there was no measure of time, until the power lines appeared.

I remembered someone once telling me that if you have to go under something through a gap, judge only the nearest possible distance for the left wing to clear, forget about the right, and concentrate on height. Less to think about.

Then I saw the telephone lines just beyond.

There wasn't much thinking left to do, and a big open patch of back yard behind a smallholding homestead right in front.

I don't remember getting much help from Paul, but then he was sitting in tandem behind me during that nose high mushing flight, and the perspex covered with light drizzle. I don't think he ever knew just how much trouble we were in. Then again, if he were writing this he might have an entirely different version.

I pushed the nose down over the roof, was aware that the wheels just clipped the tiles, and yanked back for a high-speed stall (high speed being a relative term in this instance). The nose pitched up, and we hit the ground hard enough for the undercarriage to split sideways, skidding a short distance until the left wing collided with a small fir tree. This spun the aircraft so it slid backwards into a rock wall, tail first, and as a result the tail section and fuselage absorbed all the shock.

Paul was the first with the presence of mind to ask if I was ok. I had been feverishly investigating just this, with some anxiety, and was able to confirm not a scratch.

He suggested that I try and contact the tower on the radio. It was then that I discovered that the master switch was off. So was the fuel. I don't remember consciously doing this, and it just goes to show how those ab-initio disciplines can be inculcated into your subconscious.

We staggered out of the cockpit, and I dazedly tried to come to terms with the enormity of what had happened.

How was I going to explain this tangled mess to six eager new aircraft owners, so recently coerced, so soon deprived? Had John managed to arrange hull insurance? Would they pay out? (Yes he had, - that morning. Yes they did, less the excess, which demonstrates that there **are** honourable insurers out there).

My addled brain was beginning to register that there was an apparently excited lady standing at the back door of the homestead, and that she might have cause to be somewhat surprised at such an abrupt arrival of an aircraft in her back garden. I focused my numbed senses, and it eventually penetrated the cerebral mist that she had just yelled; **"Now look what you idiots have done to my roses"!**

NB. The accident investigation revealed that the carb heat control cable had detached, with the carb heat full on.

Word on the grapevine disclosed that the excited lady had been the grand champion winner of the national rose show for the past three years, and the next show was imminent. Calamities are subjective.

The Cub is the safest aircraft in the world, it can just barely kill you.

Max Stanley - Northprop test pilot.

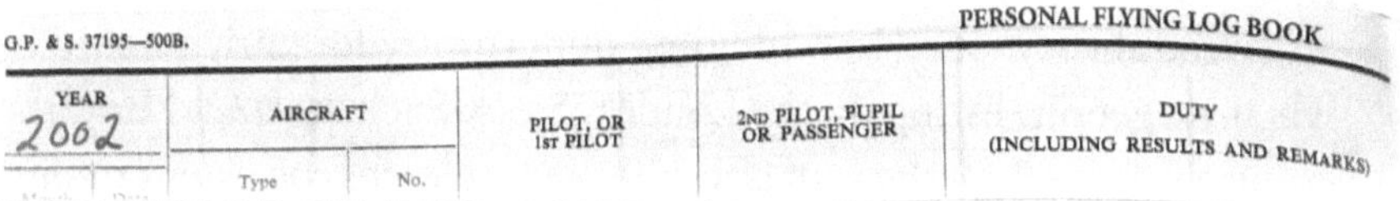

G.P. & S. 37195—500B.

PERSONAL FLYING LOG BOOK

YEAR	AIRCRAFT		PILOT, OR 1ST PILOT	2ND PILOT, PUPIL OR PASSENGER	DUTY (INCLUDING RESULTS AND REMARKS)
2002	Type	No.			

THE COCKROACH AND CONFUSION

He was one of the new-wave cockroaches that crawl out from oak-paneled offices in London, and other parts of the first world, to forage in the mineral pantries of developing nations.

This is where they identify, and then wine and dine the relevant new-order political appointee for grants of mineral concessions. This would often entail jetting the fellow 'back home' to meet prospective investors, and thence to the 'Old Club' for after dinner port and cigars.

They do this under the banner of titles such as Global Africa Minerals Exploration and Development Corporation (GAMED). The idea is to tout the

politico, and the concessions in order to seduce old money into buying shares in an extraordinary, once-in-a-life time opportunity for enrichment: "Especially when we get our listing on the London Stock Exchange, Old Boy, the price is going to go through the roof after the market learns the extent of our mineral portfolio and potential. You'll look awfully silly if you miss this one."

Enticing the gullible old money also helps to buy the right political influence for hushing things up if the crap hits the cartwheel, like it did in the DRC. (Democratic Republic of Congo.)

I think the idea is then for the cockroach to sell soon after the listing. 'Profit taking' is what they call it, but it really should be called 'theft by false pretences.'

What has this got to do with flying you might ask? Well it is just to give you some background to this particular cockroach who had solicited the services of a freelance pilot, already doing some work for a similar organization. Besides flying, the pilot would be a useful source of information regarding what the opposition cockroach was up to.

One of the pilot's first tasks was to fly a gravity separation processing expert to a place the cockroach had named 'Ace' in Namibia, where GAMED had secured some new concessions.

He was given a credit card for expenses, and told to get the processing expert up to the local airfield for pick up at 10:30 sharp two days later, in order to meet on site with the geologist who would be motoring down from Windhoek.

The pilot pulled out his map and quickly found it; Aus, only 45 minutes flying time west of Keetmanshoop off the main road to Luderitz.

It was agreed with the processor that they would fly up the following afternoon, spend the night in Upington, South Africa, where they would clear immigration out early the next morning, and fly in to Keetmanshoop, Namibia, so as to make their 10:30 rendezvous.

All went according to plan. The pilot and the processor found themselves sitting at a lonely strip in the barren Namibian moonscape at precisely 10:30.

Still there after 12:30, the processor pondered aloud that perhaps they might be at the wrong place, which prompted the pilot, somewhat nervously to look again at his map, and to discover with horror, that there was a place called Auas 60 nautical miles to the north east.

They were soon winging their way.

On arrival at Auas, a few low level passes revealed the strip to be knee high with scrub bush, and obviously long abandoned. They decided they had no choice but to return to Aus.

All this time the geologist had been sitting in his car at the airfield at Uis, 350 nautical miles to the north.

Ace, Aus, Auas, Uis.........Eeish! But then, as everyone knows, those Brits have difficulty pronouncing their own language.

<u>Author's note:</u>

Eeish; a useful South African expletive with any of the following definitions;

With eyes downcast, and slow shaking of the head; Deep, sympathetic empathy.

With hands clasping each side of head, eyes wide; Incredulous disbelief.

With arms akimbo, hands on hips, with grin; Shared humour at preposterous situation.

Pretty much any meaning interpreted according to utterer's body language.

The four things of least use to a pilot are the runway behind him, the sky above him, the air in his fuel tanks and the wrong airfield.

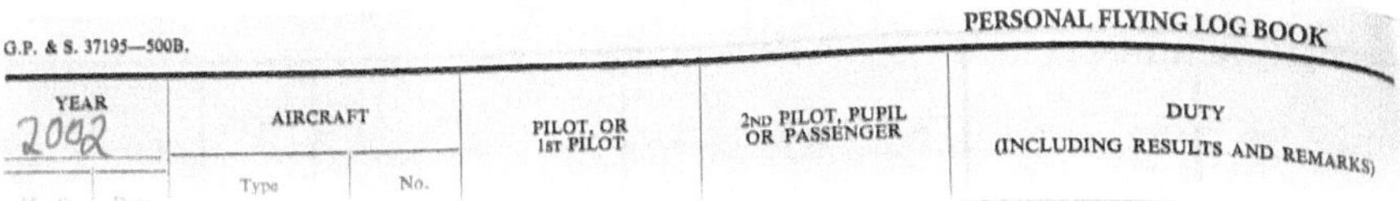
G.P. & S. 37195—500B.

PERSONAL FLYING LOG BOOK

YEAR 2002	AIRCRAFT		PILOT, OR 1ST PILOT	2ND PILOT, PUPIL OR PASSENGER	DUTY (INCLUDING RESULTS AND REMARKS)
	Type	No.			

QNH

Disconsolate, perplexed and apprehensive, we were sipping a cold beer on the verandah of a Keetmanshoop B & B that had been recommended by a helpful taxi driver solicited at the airport.

This was after our return from having spent most of the day sitting amidst the barren dunes of south west Namibia, at a remote airstrip next to a gravel road that traversed the Namib Desert between Keetmanshoop and Luderitz.

Other than a short reconnaissance flight to establish that we were not supposed to be at Auas, a similarly named abandoned airstrip north east of our isolated vigil, our only respite had been a five kilometer walk under the baking sun to the little village shown as Aus.

How that sparse village justified a local airstrip was a mystery.

We had nevertheless been able to purchase a Coke and hard bun at one of the five buildings, one of which promised fuel from a single hand pump out front, as well as professing to be a hotel.

It was after 14:00 when we returned to the aircraft, to irrefutably confront that we had somehow got it wrong. Our arranged 10:30 pick-up that morning a no-show, we were clearly not where we were supposed to be.

Following our return to Keetmanshoop, and explaining our predicament to the B & B owner, he had proposed that perhaps we should be at a mining town up in the North called Uis.

We hadn't finished our first beer when we noticed the manager hurriedly waddling towards us, declaring that someone was asking for me on the phone. This before a cellular network was available.

At first I was incredulous that we had been tracked down, until it turned out this was simply an expedient of phoning our departure airport in South Africa and tracking our flight plan from there. After using a number of colourful expletives to demonstrate his displeasure, our infuriated patron said that he had arranged for the geologist that we were supposed to meet at 10:30 that morning, to stay overnight, and that it was imperative that we were at Uis before 07:00, because he then had other appointments in Windhoek for the afternoon.

I agreed that he could depend on us being there.

The alternative would mean having to personally shoulder the cost of this debacle. I just didn't have that kind of money, and the rationale for all this was to get enough utilization to pay the installments and the upkeep for the Cherokee Six.

A search in my flying case for suitable aeronautical charts revealed 'Keetmanshoop'; extending only up to Latitude 24, and then; 'Kalahari' and 'Tsumeb' previously used for trips into Botswana, but they both margined along longitude 19, far to the east of my required route.

Why would I need any other map on departure, when my destination was well within the map that I had originally used for my flight plan?

The ever helpful B & B manager was able to furnish us with a detailed Shell road map depicting roads, rivers, towns and of course yellow shell emblems clearly denoting fuel stations, but nothing to show relief or spot heights. Scrutiny quickly revealed 'Uis'; right up to the north east, next to a crossed pick and shovel mining pictogram.

This turned out to be 350 nautical miles away, and represented three hours flying time. Departure would have to be before 04:00!

Once again the Manager came to our aid, assuring us that it would be no less than a pleasure to wake us up at three, and take us out to the airport after a mug of coffee. What a kind and accommodating person he turned out to be.

Our initial inbound flight approach and landing on the previous day had been on the 'unmanned airfield frequency', after relentless calls to Keetmanshoop Approach Control had proved fruitless. We had learned after landing from the immigration officer (who was also the acting customs and excise official) that the duty air traffic controller had gone in pursuit of his girlfriend, who had run away after a domestic row two days before. It was not known when he would return to duty. His co-controller had been summoned to Windhoek to attend a one week training course.

It transpired that the customs official was also indulging an impromptu and unauthrised absence on some personal agenda. Just another normal day for an international airport in Africa.

The subsequent departure and return flights had all been conducted on the general and unmanned airport frequencies, so there would be little chance of having to comply with any ATC (Air Traffic Control) formalities, and I was confident that we would be abandoned to our own devices.

Not having to file IFR (Instrument Flight Rules) was a real convenience, since I did not hold an instrument rating.

Obtaining my instrument rating had long been an ambition of mine, and some two years previously I had paid for a ground course at a local flight training institution. Since then I had accumulated just under five hours of simulator time, and nearly 13 hours cockpit time under instruction. Other than that, I had established a fanatical habit of pretending that I was flying IFR behind my Foggles for every VFR (Visual Flight Rules) flight, practising for the day when my ability would hopefully be tested.

This practice had become a comfortable zone where the world was shut out. It was a haven requiring my concentration and a discipline that allowed escape from the realities that would otherwise invade my mind.

During the night, the hot dry easterlies had been replaced by the south west wind, one of the strongest of any coastal desert, the consequent upwelling bringing in an immense fog that had penetrated inland for several hundred kilometers.

Our 3:20 arrival back at the airport was met with a gentle swirl of foggy

droplets, and ten meters visibility.

I started the motor and taxied to an airport security light where I carried out a very careful pre-flight, checking samples from each of the four tanks as well as the central sump. A forced landing at night with no visibility was not an attractive consideration.

Setting the runway elevation required winding the altimeter subscale through about four hundred feet to establish runway QNH (Value of atmospheric pressure when known airfield elevation is set on altimeter), indicating just how much the pressure had increased during the night.

The single landing light under the nose cone lit up the taxiway center-line, and I slowly taxied, with slight directional variations to make sure the flight instruments were responding correctly, to the 04 runway threshold. A 180° swing on to the runway centerline revealed this in the single landing light beam for a distance of about 200 meters. There was no reference for sky, and only blackness for where the stars might be.

Engine run up and final cockpit checks included a very careful runway heading set on the DI (gyroscopic Direction Indicator).

With the hollow gut sensation that only comes with purposefully breaking the law at great risk, I finally pushed the throttle and pitch levers all the way home, and immediately deflected my eyes to the instruments; revs sufficient, airspeed increasing, artificial horizon direction steady, ball dead center, airspeed 40, direction steady, airspeed 60, direction steady, V1, and rotate, a few wobbles corrected with aileron and rudder, and she settled into a steady climb.

Climb established checks scan airspeed 95, scan attitude two bars above brown, scan altimeter, climbing through 3,500 feet scan AI (gyroscopic Attitude Indicator), and my familiar pattern was established.

All the readouts in the green and on the mark, a familiar and comfortable place, and I was soon enveloped back into the warm womb of my safe cocoon.

Almost all the flying I have done in central and South Africa has been at either 6,500 or 7,500 feet in visual flight rule compliance with the semicircular flight rule, and only seldom have I filed for flight levels higher than this for weather or comfort. The only time terrain has been a consideration for a VFR flight has been over the Eastern mountain ranges bordering the Great Rift Valley.

Other than on their Eastern regions, South Africa, Zimbabwe, Zambia have nothing over 6,000ft.

The highest peak in neighboring Botswana is something a little less than 4,900 feet. Anyone familiar with the continent profile knows that it rises up steeply to mountains flanking the great rift valley in the east, levels off to central plateaux, and then recedes towards the west, which comprises mostly desert, and subsides into dunes before the Atlantic Ocean coast.

A search flanking the section of required track on the Keetmanshoop aeronautical chart had revealed nothing higher than 5,400 feet. I never considered that there might be anything higher than 6,000 feet, and had been pondering whether I should plan for Flight Level 65 for VFR, or FL80 to appear compliant with IFR in case Windhoek approach should pick me up on their radar, and opted for the latter.

Better to be discovered as an unfiled IFR flight in IMC (Instrument Meteorological Conditions), than an unfiled VFR flight in IMC. I had never had to proffer my license as proof of my capabilities in over 30 years of flying, and was confident that a request for submitting an IFR flight plan en-route would be accepted without protest.

I transitioned at 5,000 feet, setting 1013.2 (standard barometric pressure) on the altimeter subscale, and was relieved to note that the needle wound up around 400 feet that I wouldn't have to actually climb through. I would be at my flight level sooner, rather than later.

Leveling off at flight level 80, I set up power for best cruise, fine-tuned the mixture with the exhaust gas temperature gauge as reference, then eased back on the yoke for 200 foot climb above my flight level, and trimmed attitude a hair for nose down. I knew the lift generated from the slight increase in speed would translate into level flight 'on the step', and that that she would finally settle at the required level for best possible trim at optimal speed. I didn't want to arrive any later that I needed to.

My planning had abandoned any reference to the limited aeronautical chart in favour of the road map now on my lap, and in between my constant scan pattern, was attempting to associate the fuzzed conglomeration of lights sporadically, and only vaguely discernible through the blackness, with the names of towns shown along the route. The flight had settled into a seemingly languorous steady growl of the big old 300 horse power Lycoming unwaveringly pulling us through the cold tranquil gloom.

I looked across at Peter, the gravity separation engineer, wondering if he might be a useful collaborator for guessing our position in relation to the town names, but he was fast asleep, and had obviously happily abandoned his safety to my capable hands. I had neglected to mention to him that I was not qualified to be doing this.

We had been flying for an hour and forty five minutes when there was a sudden roiling, buffeting sensation, followed by what can only be described as a whooshing drag and release, accompanied by a high frequency judder. I sensed Peter jerk awake, and felt the hair on the back of my neck and arms stand up with a tingling sensation. This was like nothing I had ever experienced. It was something more than just turbulence.

I instinctively pulled back on the yoke and applied power for climb while my brain struggled to come to terms with the sensation we had just experienced.

"What the hell was that" asked Peter. I hesitated before answering; "Just turbulence". But I was thinking; "Like dragging the undercarriage through tall grass or bushes"!

I had been completely fazed by this experience, and decided that there would be no harm climbing to the next level, and 10 minutes later we were established at Flight Level 10.

The flight continued as previously with the only distraction being fuel tank changes and the new manifestation of sporadic star clumps appearing through dissipating mist.

At well after 06:00, there was only the slightest lightening of the vapour laden air to the east, and my new anxiety was occupied with wondering if the sun would ever appear. The sole dawning so far had been the realization that this

far east in mid-winter, daylight was going to be a lot later than expected.

As the light gradually dawned, so the fog dissipated, and at 06:30 I commenced my descent.

The long shadows shortened and the fog dispersed in rapid symphony with our descent. I was fascinated by the craggy black rock formations now appearing silhouetted out of the flat desert sand north east of us and astounded by a solitary circular dome shaped megalith protruding out of the flat sand plain. It seemed to tower above our current 6,500 foot altitude at our 11 o'clock.

I had never been here. I never expected this. I thought deserts were all undulating flatness, with the odd scattered cactus tree.

It was some months later that I needed to purchase the Windhoek map for a planned trip there, and again some months after that, before I finally charted our flight for this trip. I suppose there was a definite reluctance to confront just what a stupid and reckless pilot I really was. Validation of what I suspected would seriously challenge the high opinion I had of my ability.

And there it was. Right in the middle of our required track. Gamsberg peak, spot heighted at 7,700 feet. Just ten millibars of pressure below our flight level standard pressure setting.

The assumed turbulence we had experienced could only have been from severe ground effect drag, generated from critical proximity to terrain. We must have been within a few feet from impacting the Gamsberg pinnacle.

I saw Peter frequently during the months following this flight, and even spent some weeks with him on a mining operation in the north of Zimbabwe. We became good friends. It all came to an end when I was arrested on suspicion of smuggling by the Zimbabwean Central Intelligence Organization, and then released after someone I suspected did not have my best interests as a priority, intervened to use his influence to affect my release! It was all very puzzling. I was realizing that I was out of my depth, involuntarily involved in a world of greed, deceit and intrigue, and decided that my flying for dubious mining operations should abruptly end.

You generally don't get to hear of accidents that should have happened, only of those that did. If I ever bump into Peter again, should I tell him just how close he had been to a sudden and violent death? He would have a story to tell his grandchildren, and could perhaps even qualify for the TV series; "I shouldn't be Alive".

Nah. Don't think so. It might get out, and I will be in trouble with the CAA. This one will have to remain with just you and me.

Note: The domed Megalith referred to just 30 kilometers north east of Uis is Brandberg, topping at 8,461 feet.

One day you will walk out to an aeroplane knowing that it will be your last flight, or you will walk out to an aeroplane not knowing that it will be your last flight.

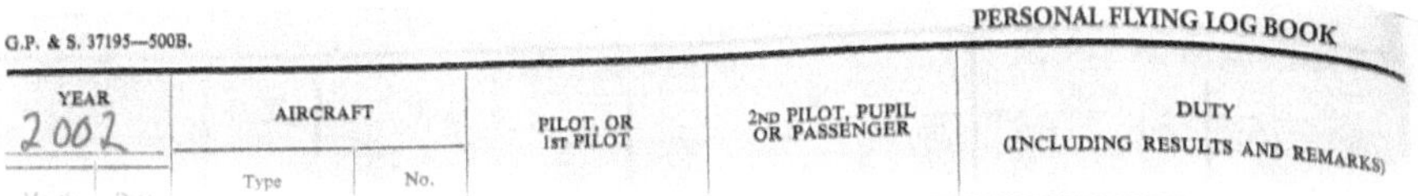
G.P. & S. 37195—500B.

PERSONAL FLYING LOG BOOK

YEAR	AIRCRAFT		PILOT, OR 1st PILOT	2nd PILOT, PUPIL OR PASSENGER	DUTY (INCLUDING RESULTS AND REMARKS)
2002	Type	No.			

AIR CRASH INVESTIGATION

She looked up at the ceiling, and rolled her eyes.

"Oh God, here we go again" she said, loud enough to make sure he would hear her, while pretending to be talking to herself.

They had been married for three years now, just long enough to have started carping at each other, and were expecting their first child. She was crocheting a blue blanket for the baby's cot. They had been told that it was going to be a boy.

He was watching "Air Crash Investigation" on TV. She would much rather be watching a movie that was showing on another channel.

She was reacting after he had exclaimed, "I can't believe they can be so stupid!"

He looked at her with some exasperation; "Can't they understand that the guy in the tower is just confirming the information being relayed from the equipment on board the aircraft?"

"Yes, yes Dear, but they are commercial pilots, and you are just a Private Pilot. I'm sure they know a little more than you do," she responded a little patronizingly.

Dennis had qualified for his PPL four years earlier. It had taken him about a year to do so while he scratched to find the spare cash to cover the cost of his training. He had only qualified just one month before he had first met her, and during their courtship, proudly flew her away over weekends as part of his agenda for impressing her. She had professed then, to be dazzled by this

amazing talent and ability.

Of course this rose-tinted adulation had been somewhat tempered by the passing of time, and the fact that Dennis was now successfully ensnared. Her previous ardour had been replaced by a mild resentment of the time Dennis spent at the flying club over weekends, as well as the drain on their finances, particularly now that the baby was on the way.

He looked at her, feeling his ire rising. She was emasculating the very essence of his being.

Flying was his absolute passion, and he was on the point of uttering an angry rejoinder when he realized the futility of this. There was no arguing a point with someone who had no interest in flying, and even less in things technical.

Dennis was rocketing up the corporate ladder, and his financial status was significantly improved from the days when he was first learning to fly. He was now harboring dreams of buying his own Cessna 182, and endlessly fantasizing family weekends away in the bush, or at one of the tropical Mozambican islands.

He had long established a resolve to practise every possible emergency procedure for at least one hour every month, and avidly read every aircraft accident report so as to determine the best response if he were ever exposed to the same circumstance. He was committed to being the best he could be, and resolute that he would never become a 'Pilot Error' statistic.

"I bet they are going to find that there was something blocking the static vent."

"If you say so, Dear" she retorted with an air of long-suffering indifference.

His attention was now back on the TV screen where utter chaos reigned in the cockpit, with a multitude of simultaneous warnings all blaring and competing for attention, the most demanding being that ominous: "Terrain, Too Low, Terrain, Too Low, Terrain, Too Low, Terrain," pitched at just the right monotone to defy being ignored, and send the ultimate fear trigger! 'PULL UP'!

The Boeing 757 central on-board computer was sending a multitude of hysterically contradictory messages; 'over speed' followed by 'stall warning' whilst showing conflicting air speed and altimeter values, all blurting and beeping in frenzied discord.

Shortly after take-off all three altimeters had failed to function correctly, showing lagging increase in altitude, whilst the air speed indicators were indicating an exponentially increasing airspeed. The captain and first officer had tried to counteract every indication with the flight controls, sending the aircraft into frantic pitch oscillations, whilst becoming more and more baffled and alarmed.

They had then engaged the assistance of the departure aerodrome ATC to obtain ground readouts of their actual values for altitude, and ground speed, not cognitive that the altitude being relayed was sourced from the aircraft's onboard transponder.

Dennis involuntarily found himself leaping up in front of his favorite TV chair, in agitated frustration. He had identified that the malfunctioning flight instruments were all only those that were pressure impelled, and wanted to shout "For FUCK'S sake, ignore them. Fly the FUCKING aeroplane!"

"Just establish a known power and trim setting for climb, then level flight until you sort out a plan for a glide-slope approach and landing! Then adjust descent with power and trim. The attitude indicator is working fine, for fuck's sake!"

He desperately wanted to save the lives of the 90 people on board.

Instead, the TV screen showed the aircraft plunging into the Pacific Ocean, and all on board perished.

The crash investigation revealed that one of the cleaners had neglected to remove duct tape placed over the static vents to protect them from moisture whilst the aircraft was being cleaned.

In any event, of course there was just no way Dennis would have been able to save the souls on board.

He was after all, just a private pilot.

When you are faced with a crisis; Aviate! Navigate! Communicate!

G.P. & S. 37195—500B. PERSONAL FLYING LOG BOOK

YEAR	AIRCRAFT		PILOT, OR 1ST PILOT	2ND PILOT, PUPIL OR PASSENGER	DUTY (INCLUDING RESULTS AND REMARKS)
2067	Type	No.			

MAYDAY

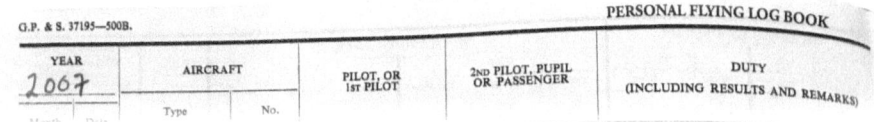

Cliff was so pleased at having qualified for his instrument rating just three months previously, that even on a clear day with no inclement weather predicted, he would file for IFR.

Because he could.

This is why he happened to be flying at 21,000 feet when an initially barely audible high pitched whistle began to pervade the steady familiar whine of the turbocharger. Alerted, his hand went instinctively to the throttle control knob, winding out the friction lock, and when the whine suddenly developed into a screeching crescendo, he pulled, a nano second before the screech progressed to a grinding convulsion.

He prayed that he had prevented a cascade of metal shards being sucked into the big Teledyne Continental's cylinders.

Aware of the passenger in the seat next to him suddenly jerking erect, he proclaimed, "It's all right guys, it's going to be OK."

This while applying a firm, smooth pull back on the yoke, and going through his emergency rote: "Convert speed to height; Trim for glide; Direction wind (there were no visible references, but he knew this to be 10 knots from port, and behind), Find field."

He had briefly considered holding the yoke back until the propeller had stopped wind milling so as to lessen the likelihood of tiny pieces of metal finding their way past the induction butterfly, but decided that the resulting loss of height, possibility of developing a spin, and the effect on his already

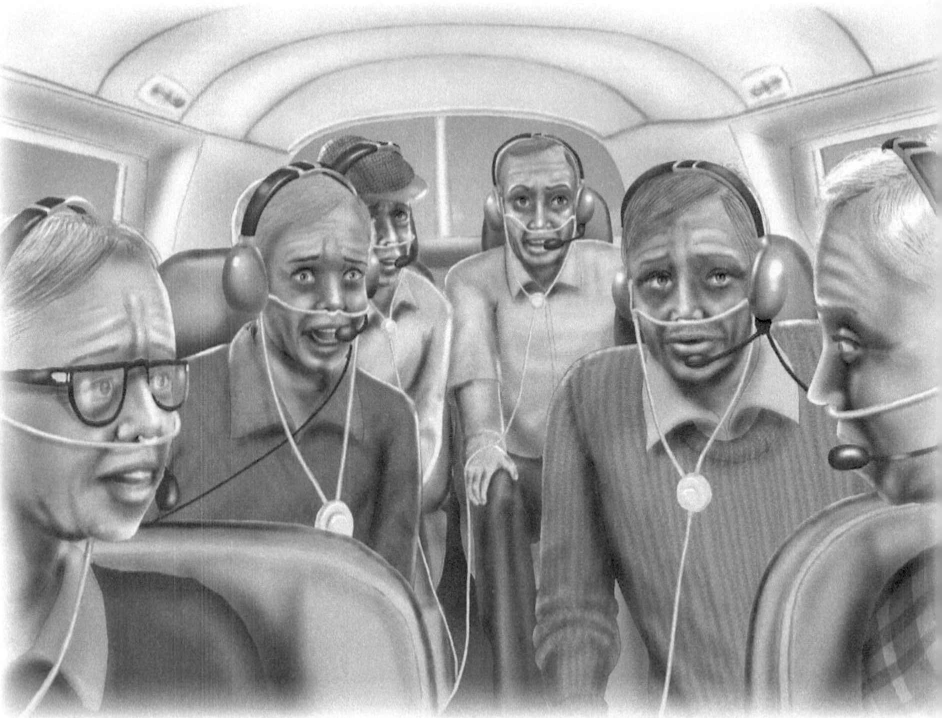

frightened passengers would be a dangerous trade-off.

He jabbed the GPS 'nearest' button, which revealed three alternatives. The closest, Belfast, was only ten nautical miles behind but into wind. They had only just flown over this some four minutes previously. Cliff had landed there before on a trout fishing foray. Elevated at 6,500 feet, it was a rough, sloping, dirt strip with a water tower and tall trees on the approach into wind.

Next closest Carolina: elevation 5,400 feet, and 30 nautical miles to the south/south east.

But the third nearest was his destination airfield, Nelspruit at 2,900 feet and downwind, just 40 nautical miles to run, probably presented an equal, if not better, prospect.

Could he make it?

A glance at the altimeter revealed he was only now descending back through his flight level of 21,000 feet.

A quick mental calculation determined that he had a comfortable 18,000 feet, and the Garmin was showing his ETA in twenty six minutes at his current indicated 86 knots, and ground speed a tad above 90.

Suddenly confident, and without further thought, he thumbed his prestle switch. "**Mayday, mayday, mayday**, Johannesburg Information, this is November Poppa Golf reporting catastrophic engine failure, and initiating emergency landing."

Only after the slightest pause: "November Poppa Golf, understand catastrophic engine failure, have you identified a suitable emergency field?"

"Affirmative, we intend proceeding to our planned destination, Nelspruit."

"Roger November Poppa Golf, no reported traffic for descent, contact Nelspruit Approach on 118 decimal 8, and good luck, out."

Cliff did as he was told, and was assured by Nelspruit that they would clear the circuit for a straight in approach on runway 22, and that he should call 'field in sight'.

Only now did Cliff turn to his five passengers, to be met with identical, white faced, big eyed expressions of abject terror.

He assured them that all was going to be just fine, explaining the circumstances, and what would be expected of them when he made the calls. This at least had the apparent outcome that the previous dread was being replaced by a general resignation to the fate that was awaiting them.

He then focused on dealing with their situation.

He yanked the propeller control knob out for full course pitch, felt the subtle surge of acceleration, and cursed for not having done this sooner. The reduced drag would extend his glide by at least two minutes.

Now passing through Flight Level 19 representing 16,000 feet altitude, a glance at the VSI indicated a descent of just over 700 feet per minute, and he knew he needed to improve on this.

His five burly passengers were on their way to a golfing weekend with shared suitcases and all their golf equipment which had computed to being just under Maximum All Up Weight, but the Centre of Gravity was right in the middle of the envelope top line.

The heavy load would flatten, and extend the glide path if he applied the optimum air speed. Cliff tweaked the elevator trim wheel a tad forward, noted the increase of indicated airspeed to around 90, and the flickering VSI (Vertical Speed Indicator) needle settled on 690 feet per minute descent rate.

The Garmin had reverted to run time of 26 minutes, and a new ground speed of 92 knots. Cliff punched the numbers into the calculator on his lap. 26 x 690 = 17,940 feet. A new margin of just under 2,000 feet at the threshold.

He radioed Nelspruit requesting QNH (Atmospheric Pressure at Destination elevation), and when he dialed this in, the needle added another 200 feet of altitude. Even better. Cliff felt the tension melt away, and a new feeling of almost elation replace it. Piece of old takkie. It was going to be OK.

Cliff's ordeal was going to stretch over a torturous 30 minutes.

A lot can happen in 30 minutes. As soon as Cliff had made his emergency call, the tower had alerted the emergency services for a fire engine and ambulance. They had promptly responded, and made their way down to predetermined positions on the runway verge.

One of the emergency personnel had phoned his friend who worked as a reporter for the Nelspruit Post, and told him that there was an aircraft approaching with a dead engine, and he better get to the airport fast if he wanted to cover the prang.

There were others who had been listening in to traffic radio patter on hand sets.

The police were notified, and felt it necessary to send two vehicles to the scene of an imminent crash with sirens blaring.

A stream of workers at first trickled, and then gushed out of hangars and other buildings at the airport, making their way down to the open ground for best view of the approaching catastrophe.

Cell phone screens lit up as the word spread to a flickering daylight galaxy across the small Lowveld town, and vehicles started filtering on to the single access road to the airfield. It was not long before this conduit became a congested jam.

Dear reader, this might be a good time to wipe and flush, and continue at the next sitting.

Cliff and his passengers had departed from Grand Central between Johannesburg and Pretoria at just after 10:00 for what was to be a short 55 minute flight. Even shorter if the mild tail wind had remained a constant. The turbo charger had disintegrated 40 minutes into the flight, and by the time they were now descending through 13,000 feet altitude, they had been in the air for nearly an hour. The cool crisp morning of their departure was evolving into sultry hot Lowveld midday.

The light prevailing north east breeze was converting to anabatic south west caused by the escarpment slope from the Lowveld to the Highveld plateau. Cliff had been gazing out at the relentless view of jagged tree covered granite koppies which characterized the ground below in every direction for fifty miles, and shuddered at the thought of even considering having to decide how he might try and put the plane down if there was no alternative.

A sudden positive G lift jerked his attention back to the instruments and he noted a rise of some 300 feet on the altimeter, before the VSI needle settled back to indicating a steady 690 feet per minute, and the ASI settle back at just under 90 kts. It was then that a glance at the Garmin now showed a ground speed of only 85kts. The wind had veered to the front.

Cliff quickly recalculated; Distance 27 nautical miles to run, with 19 minutes run time x 690 feet a minute descent rate = 13,110. His anticipated 2,000 threshold height had been reduced to a mere 110 feet in the last 10 minutes.

It was now becoming mildly bumpy, and the creaking protests of the airframe in the silence, only broken by the shrilly intermittent monotonous beep from the undercarriage warning, seemed to be portentous. The next air pocket sent them soaring 400 feet, before they were then plummeted to a net loss of 500.

Cliff's stomach knotted with anxiety. He was now desperately regretting his decision to continue to Nelspruit instead of opting for one of the other alternatives. Had it been Belfast, they would have been on the ground by now.

During the next ten minutes his nerves had been run ragged by the repetitive thermals and down draughts resulting from the rapidly warming air.

There was no way now to determine the final outcome. In spite of all his efforts to appear imperturbable, Cliff's anxiety had permeated the cabin, and while not a word had been uttered, each of the passengers was made aware of the ragged breathing of his neighbour, whilst struggling to come to terms with his own inner turmoil.

With nine minutes to run, they still had 6000 ft. in hand, and a distance of 13 nautical miles, when the airfield became vaguely visible through the haze.

At the same time, the tiny spot in the western sky identifying the approaching plane became visible to those with sharpest vision, and there was an upwelling of excitement accompanied by fingers pointing, reaching fever pitch as the little dot grew inexorably bigger.

"There he is, there, there!"

"No way is he going to make it," was a popular opinion, while the crowd concertinaed toward the best view, the tension mounting with every passing minute.

Cliff now shared this viewpoint. Heart beating somewhere in his dry throat, his trained eye left him with no doubt that he was going to land short.

He was rationalizing his final options. He would approach flapless all the way to stretch the glide as far into the impact as possible. He would delay extending the undercarriage until the very last opportunity to avert the drag that this would generate, and land wheels up if this was going to be in the trees short of the runway undershoot. He would crank in full flap, and lift the nose for slowest possible impact speed.

It was only now that it dawned that he still had a motor!

He had closed it down. It had not failed on its own accord. He could restart this, and could hope perhaps to use it to climb as much as 500 feet, even while the broken turbocharger pieces were destroying the pistons and valves. This gave him new courage. He turned the fuel back on to LEFT TANK, and selected FULL RICH.

Expecting even more height loss when initiating a gentle right turn through 140 degrees to line up with the runway, his hand went out to set the throttle for start, but was deflected down by an unexpected G force. The airframe shuddered and creaked its protest, and Cliff saw the VSI needle flick up to vertical for several seconds, before settling back down below the zero line.

They had soared 300 feet in a thermal just before the 04 stop way threshold.

Miraculously, the glide slope now appeared to point to the threshold numbers.

With only 100 feet above ground, Cliff selected wheels down, and toggled the flap switch for 30 degrees. He noted 3 greens, undercarriage down and locked, even as he eased back for the flare at 60 knots. A few seconds later, the tyres whispered their gentle meeting with the tar.

Behind him John uttered a loud sob of relief, and Fred exclaimed "Well done Cliff! Well done. Thank God, thank God."

Buoyed by the relief and success of their safe arrival, Cliff impetuously avoided using the brakes, and instead swerved onto the up-sloping taxiway so that the heavy big single finally came to a halt on the flat surface just before the fuel pumps. Within distance of being pushed by hand to the neatest AMO* workshop. (*Aircraft Maintenance Organization.)

Now the huge crowd were looking on in stony silence.

The much anticipated spectacle had not materialized, and there was a general atmosphere of deprivation and disappointment.

Deflated, even resentful, they slowly started to dissipate. Cheated.

The incident didn't even make mention in the local paper.

Take off is optional, Landing is compulsory

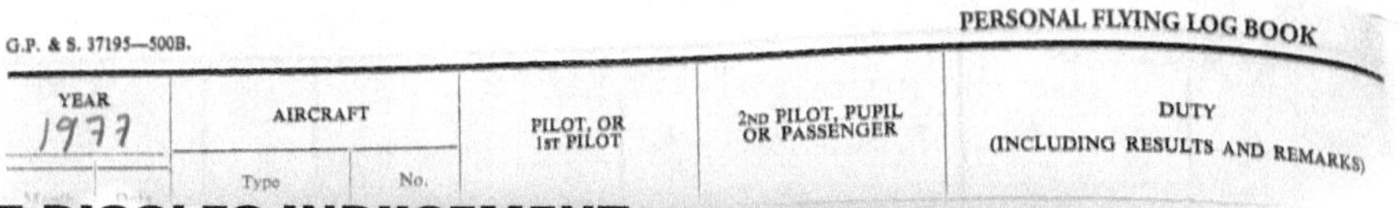

THE BIGGLES INDUCEMENT

With reverence for the poetic ability of John Gillespie Magee, who wrote this age 19, while he was in Britain with No. 412 (Fighter) squadron, Royal Canadian Airforce, flying spitfires in 1941.

"Oh! I have slipped the surly bonds of earth,

And danced the skies on laughter silvered wings;

Sunward I have climbed, and joined the tumbling mirth

Of sun split clouds, and done a hundred things

You have not dreamed of. Wheeled and soared and swung

High in the sunlit silence. Hov'ring there

I've chased the shouting wind along, and flung

My eager craft through footless halls of air.

Up, up the long, delirious burning blue

I've topped the wind swept heights with easy grace

Where never lark or even eagle flew

And while with silent lifting mind I've trod

The high untrespassed sanctity of space,

Put out my hand and touched the face of God."

What motivates us to want to fly?

Is it the desire to be as free as a bird, soar with gilded wings beyond the surly bonds of earth, perhaps touch the face of God, and certainly give the finger to the poor underprivileged bastards snarled up in the traffic below?

Or otherwise is it perhaps, to join the ranks of the glorified 'Few', and share the eminence of the derring-do exploits of Charles Lindbergh, Douglas Bader, Chuck Yeager, Neil Armstrong, but not least, be ranked by association among those to whom so much was owed by so many?

Of course to be able to bask in this warm veneration, it is necessary to learn the art of letting those around you know that you are a pilot as early as possible, in the manner of a qualified Member of Business Administration (MBA), which fraternity have a reputation for disseminating their claim to this qualification within fifteen minutes of your first acquaintance with them.

This will almost certainly result in the gratification of at least one member of your audience sighing; "I've always wanted to learn to fly," and most certainly will assure the best potential for young chicks and bored housewives to be uttering low voiced, behind palm-covered lips: "He's a PILOT, you know," in surreptitious awe.

I learned early on that for some at least, being a pilot was certainly more important than actually flying an aeroplane.

There was Peter, who paid his share of the initial capital cost, and then a third of all the subsequent expenses after we had established a three member syndicate for the purchase of a Piper Tripacer, who in three years, never progressed beyond some ab initio training. This at least allowed me the opportunity of being a part owner in my very first aeroplane, while of course Peter would be able to boast forever after that he had once owned an aircraft.

Then there was Dick and Bob, with whom I later shared a syndicated Cherokee Six 300.

Neither would fly without a qualified pilot in the right seat. Dick rarely flew the Six at all, and then succumbed to a Flight Training institute 'refresher course' just before his bi-annual flight test renewal, and came away with a freshly stamped log book allowing him to fly for another year. In the interim, on rare occasions he would ask that I fly somewhere with him. I never refused, because our syndicate badly needed the utilization revenue, and I had to endure his bumbling and clumsy handling habits, and very poor knowledge of procedures and protocols.

On each occasion I was compelled to wonder who could possibly have allowed renewal of his license.

Bob, on the other hand, never displayed anything but precise competence whenever he asked me to fly with him, except on one occasion when he let go 20 degrees of flap, before applying full power during recovery from a practice forced landing. This caused an uncomfortable amount of sink, mostly in the pit of my stomach, before a positive climb rate was established.

But this story is about John and Peggy.

John was a wealthy farmer, who had courted and married a much younger wife, generally considered by the local community to be his trophy.

He was quick to make my acquaintance soon after I arrived in the district, and I was given cause to wonder if this was not because he had learned, somehow, that I was a pilot.

He owned his very own Cherokee 180, and I was soon educated to the fact that both he and his young wife were qualified private pilots, and that he had sponsored her flight training. I am uncertain whether this sponsorship was before, or after they were married.

I also quickly learned that neither of them would fly anywhere without an alternative pilot in the right hand seat for reassurance, and wondered why anyone would spend so much money owning and maintaining such an expensive item, without the fevered passion for its unfettered use at the least excuse. It didn't suffice that they could just fly with each other for reassurance, and I wondered if this was not because of a fear of the humiliation they might feel if they were jointly exposed to some incident.

Being an aircraft owner did however allow for them to be sitting amongst the other five or six wealthy farmers who owned their own aircraft, swapping stories in their corner of the pub.

My arrangement for being an accompanying pilot in those days was that I fly PIC (Pilot in Charge), and log the hours for one of the legs, in or outbound. I don't remember ever not being available. I needed the practice and the hours.

I only flew with Peggy on two occasions, and was surprised at just how much prompting and encouragement she seemed to need. This was gladly given, because she really was a lovely looking woman. Her fragility was somehow sensed by Pat, a somewhat irascible retired commercial airline captain, now farmer, who insinuated that she was unfairly qualified because she was a good-looking blond.

He set out to prove this by asking her to explain, in front of all of us, the difference between the angle of incidence and the angle of attack. She was dumbfounded by the question, and I was embarrassed because I wished she was able to answer, and this was on the verandah of my home, where we were sitting with sundowners in hand after my two year old son's birthday party.

John, on the other hand, was very capable, if a little ponderous, and there was no need for him to mistrust his own ability.

However, this he did, and it was as a consequence that he phoned one day to ask whether I would accompany him on a flight to Milibizi, a bush strip about 240 nautical miles to the West, on the shore of Lake Kariba. He had been asked if he would go and fetch Will and Lorna who needed to return home after a short stay up there, where Will's uncle ran a hunting lodge. It was a round trip of just under 500 hundred miles, and we planned to re-fuel at Kariba on the return journey.

John suggested that I fly the first leg from Centenary to Milibizi, and I entertained us by flying through clumps of stable fair weather cumulus intermittently scattered along the route. I loved the sensation of heading at exponentially increasing speed toward an apparently rock hard towering blob of white, to be swallowed into a blind world of swirling grey, which then rapidly lightened wispily again into a world of brilliant blue.

After touching down with featherlike delicacy on the hard gravel runway, the Cherokee suddenly became a wildly oscillation bronco as soon as the nose wheel touched the ground. Applying brakes only served to worsen the violent vacillation of the nose from side to side, accompanied by a screeching, clanging grinding noise. I instinctively cut the motor.

When we finally came to a stop in the middle of a cloud of dust, in the middle of the runway, the silence was deafening.

Will and Lorna, together with Will's Uncle, had witnessed this from a pick-up truck parked to one side, and soon joined us to contemplate the cause of our spectacular and somewhat frightening arrival. It was discovered that the axle for the nose wheel, which comprises a rod inserted through a tube with spacers to lock nuts on each side of the fork had somehow, incredibly, become dismantled. The nut and inner tube spacer on one side was missing, and the wheel was left dangling on the loose tube. Whether this occurred shortly after take-off or during the flight was a puzzle, but now of only academic interest. Inspection of the propeller blade tips revealed that they had not come into contact with the ground.

Our perplexity at the cause for our predicament was soon superseded by the need for a solution.

The logistics and difficulty for arranging for an aircraft technician to be flown out from the nearest facility nearly 300 miles away to fix the problem in the remote bush, would take days if not weeks, and the expense for this would be horrific. We were all left pondering the possible alternatives.

To a farmer, the idea that we should find a short piece of resilient wood and jam this down alongside the wheel and strap it in place to serve as a skid was not extraordinary, and was soon finessed to actually replacing the wheel altogether, with a forked branch in the shape of a wish bone.

So while Will's uncle Hans went off with the axe he always kept in his 4 x 4 to find a suitable forked branch, as well as a straight length of the right diameter to substitute for the axle from the endemic Mopane forest, Will went off to strip the bark off some re-growth Mufuti bushes we had seen on the cleared undershoot, so as to fashion rope from the inner bark.

John and I were left to dismantle the remaining lock nut with a screw driver and rock substitute for a hammer, so we could remove the wheel altogether. I could sense that John was in a state of some considerable agitation and anxiety.

John was a big burly guy, and when I suggested that I fly back so that his weight could be best used to move the center of gravity away from the nose, I saw tangible relief and gratitude flood his features. This ostensible arrangement would allow that his dignity remain unchallenged.

One of the forks of the branch that Hans had fashioned was wedged under the arch of the wheel support, and the other below the improvised wooden axle, and then bound securely in place with bush tambo (bark rope). The lower branch fork would act as the skid in place of the wheel.

So it was arranged that Will's and Lorna's suitcases should be stowed as far aft as possible. For the return flight, Will would sit in the back seat with John, and Lorna, the lightest, would be up front with me.

By putting weight on the stabilator main spar, and lifting the nose off the ground, we wheeled the Cherokee to the runway threshold, and swung it around to point down the runway center.

After start-up, pre-take-off and engine checks, I applied full power and held the yoke firmly back to reduce as much weight as possible from our now front skid. During the short roll on which it was grounded, I felt no significant difference between the contrived skid and the standard nose wheel.

In fact, after landing at Kariba Airport for re-fuelling, I relaxed the desperate discipline for using power and brakes with full deflection of the stabilator whilst taxiing to hold the nose off the ground, and at the same time using brakes and rudder for steerage, having discovered that the forked branch steered equally as well as the nose wheel used to.

After stopping at the fuel pumps, we carefully inspected our piece of stick, to note that there was only mild attrition at the tip of the grounded end of the fork; otherwise it was exactly as we had bound it.

The fuel pump attendant eyed our contrivance with mild curiosity, but made no comment. In Africa, opportunism and resourceful substitution are not considered remarkable.

The take-off, and return to Centenary went without incident, as did the landing, in spite of arriving well after dark to an unlighted runway because of the unscheduled delay. This was home. I had landed here many times, and knew the silhouette of every bush on both sides, manifest in the light of the adjacent village street lights.

Some days, later I phoned John and asked if he wanted some assistance with flying his 'plane to Mount Hampden for repair. He told me he had already arranged that the *FBO send someone out. They eventually did; nearly six weeks later. (*Fixed Base Operator.)

John now had a story for his contemporaries in their corner of the pub.

I wonder how he told it?

If you didn't learn anything from your last flight, give up flying now while you are still ahead.

www.ingramcontent.com/pod-product-compliance
Lightning Source LLC
Chambersburg PA
CBHW021411290426
44108CB00010B/476
9780620787901